EUROPEAN CORPORATE STRATEGY

European Corporate Strategy

Heading for 2000

Oliver L. Landreth

St. Martin's Press

First published in Great Britain 1992 by
THE MACMILLAN PRESS LTD
Houndmills, Basingstoke, Hampshire RG21 2XS
and London
Companies and representatives
throughout the world

A catalogue record for this book is available
from the British Library

ISBN 0-333-55835-9

Printed in Great Britain by
Antony Rowe Ltd, Chippenham, Wiltshire

First published in the United States of America 1992 by
Scholarly and Reference Division,
ST. MARTIN'S PRESS, INC.,
175 Fifth Avenue,
New York, N.Y. 10010

ISBN 0-312-07916-8

Library of Congress Cataloging-in-Publication Data
European corporate strategy : heading for 2000 / Oliver L.
Landreth.
p.   cm.
Includes index.
ISBN 0-312-07916-8
1. European Economic Community countries—Industries—Case
studies.   2. Corporations—European Economic Community countries-
-Case studies.   3. Strategic planning—European Economic Community
countries—Case studies.   I. Title.
HC240.L265   1992
338.7'4'094—dc20   91-42563
                                                            CIP

Contents

List of Tables and Figures

Tables

Figures

Company Quick Reference Table

Company	Country of origin	Products/business	Geographical area of business
CMB Packaging	France/UK	Consumer goods packaging	Europe/world
FAI, SpA.	Italy	Earth moving machines	Europe/world
European Truck mfg Industry	Europe	Truck manufacturing	World
Zust Ambrosetti, SpA.	Italy	Merchandise transport	World
Banco Comercial Português	Portugal	Consumer and corporate banking	Portugal
Amsterdam Airport Schiphol	The Netherlands	Transport services	The Netherlands
SAS Scandinavian Airlines	Scandinavia	Tourism services	World
Belfe SpA.	Italy	Clothes manufacturing	Europe/USA/Japan
The Mexx Group	The Netherlands	Clothes wholesaling	Europe
Amorim Lage, S.A.	Portugal	Food production	Portugal

Case Summaries

CMB Packaging Under the leadership of Jean-Marie Descarpentries, France's leading packaging company, Carnaud went from being a weak competitor to being Europe's 'number one' packaging conglomerate as a result of its merger with British Metal Box. Despite the difficulties associated with a merger which bridges two historically different cultures as well as diverse corporate philosophies, the new CMB is now arming itself, through new management policies and strategy options, to become the number one packaging conglomerate in the world.

FAI SpA Situated in northern Italy, the family-owned FAI (manufacturers of earth-moving equipment) 'is rapidly gaining ground so as to become a leader within its sector. Among its strategies: to go public, while forging an alliance with the world's foremost competitor within this sector, the Japanese Komatsu.

The European Truck Manufacturing Industry This case aims to provide an overview of the strategies being implemented by Europe's leading truck manufacturers as they fight against deregulation not only within their own sector, but also within their client's sectors.

Zust Ambrosetti SpA One of Europe's leading global merchandise transporters, Zust Ambrosetti believes that its future success lies in its ability to master the efficient use of market information, as well as in the creation of strategic alliances throughout Europe.

Banco Comercial Português A newcomer to the banking industry, BCP has risen in record time from being a dream of some idealistic managers to being one of Portugal's leading commercial banking institutions and a major force for change in the Portuguese economy. At the heart of its success lies its unwavering commitment to the client, as witnessed by its marketing-dominated strategy.

Amsterdam Airport Schiphol Though serving a country with a limited market base, Amsterdam Airport Schiphol aims to be one of Europe's leading hub airports for travellers from around the world by providing not just traditional airport facilities, but all the necessities that will make up a major transport centre in the year 2000.

SAS Scandinavian Airlines Repeatedly voted one of the world's best airlines in the 1980s, SAS is presently gearing up to face the aggressive competition and industry restructuring that is expected to result from the travel industry's deregulation in 1993. Its goal: to be one of the five remaining mega-carriers in Europe. Its strategy: to create strategic alliances around the world.

Belfe Clothes Well-known in Italy for its elegantly-styled sports clothes, Belfe would like to see its brand name achieve world-wide recognition. To succeed, the company is placing great emphasis on its marketing strategies and its ability to gain access to distribution channels in such key markets as the United States and Japan.

The Mexx Group Acting as a clothes wholesaler based in The Netherlands, the Mexx Group experienced a dramatic turnaround in the latter half of the 1980s and is now gaining strength to solidify its position within its chosen market niche. Among the major changes implemented towards the company's turnaround: an internal organisation and a marketing strategy that follow the classic lines of business textbooks.

Amorim Lage, S.A. As a concluding case, this chapter aims to look at the challenges and threats that family-run, medium-sized companies (the backbone of Europe's economy) are facing with the onslaught of competitors possessing a strong European or global position.

Preface

The imminent arrival of a new Europe in 1992, combined with the unprecedented events recently witnessed in Eastern Europe, have made it abundantly clear to managers and politicians alike that the future corporate battleground is no longer the United States or Japan, but, instead, Europe itself. Despite the fact that '1992' has been laboured upon *ad infinitum* by academics, politicians, students and executives, it does nevertheless provide a useful backdrop for discussion and it succeeds in bringing to light one of the major trends that is presently taking place on a world-wide scale: the ever-growing globalisation of markets coupled with increased regionalisation and hence fragmentation.

Whether or not European political unity will ever be achieved, or whether it is even desirable, it is nevertheless evident in today's leading corporations that 1992 is the logical and natural end-result of an ongoing economic process to find the most profitable and efficient means of operating across geographic borders. Many major American, as well as Japanese, corporations have long considered Europe as one market, a fact which ironically may have contributed to the ill fate of some ambitious transnational projects, as managers failed to recognise that the key to success lies not in product standardisation, but in adaptability and diversity all the while achieving standardisation in production.

Much has already been written on 'Europe 1992' and much more will undoubtedly be published. My objective in writing this book has not been to add theory to theory but, instead, to provide an insider's view of what is actually going on inside Europe's corporations as they prepare to meet the challenges of the 1990s.

What are Europe's leading managers doing to guarantee their company's survival into the twenty-first century? Are there set solutions? Are there tricks? What will be the key success factors in the years ahead? Who is the manager of the future?

The case studies found in this book are a modest attempt to help answer these questions from the point of view of the manager who must not only plan his everyday schedule, but also find the time to think of the decade we have just begun. The companies were chosen in such a way as to present the challenges being faced by managers of small or medium-sized corporations (for example, Belfe Clothes, FAI) as well as multinationals (for example, SAS Scandinavian Airlines, CMB Packaging). In addition, in the hope of gaining a more thorough understanding of what opportunities are provided by globalisation in a world as fragmented as the European Community, the geographical base of these companies stretches from the confines of Southern Europe (Portugal) to Scandinavia, passing through France, Britain, Italy and The Netherlands.

While the concept of this book arose out of the perceived lack of European case studies in business programmes, it is my hope that managers will find it of interest to learn how their colleagues in different sectors and countries perceive their respective situations.

OLIVER L. LANDRETH

Acknowledgements

I would like to take this opportunity to thank all those who facilitated the research for this book. They include:

Rui Amorim de Sousa, Consultant
E. Barulli and F. Forti, FAI SpA
Wim De Man, Manager Corporate Marketing, Amsterdam Airport Schiphol
John Drew, the European Commission, London
Giancarlo Forconi, Director, Vicenza Industrial Association
Oliver Gray, American Chamber of Commerce in Brussels
Frank de Haan
R. C. van den Heuvel and Thierry Lemane, CMB Packaging
K. Lovstuhagen, Director Corporate Communications, The SAS Group
Stefano Festa Marzotto, Belfe SpA
Dr Namorado Rosa, Banco Comercial Português
Dr Leo Sleuwagen, Professor, Katholiek Universiteit, Leuven and Erasmus University, Rotterdam
Dr Paul Verdin, Professor of Business Policy at INSEAD
John Watson, Mexx International
Ruud Wever, Amsterdam Airport Schiphol
Romano Zanolli, Zust Ambrosetti SpA

In addition, I would like to thank both SAS Scandinavian Airlines and Banco Comercial Português for their generous support in the financing of the necessary research.

1 The Challenges Ahead

INTRODUCTION

'Europe' has never been a more abstract and, simultaneously, a more concrete nomenclature than today. On the one hand, everybody recognises it as being a collection of countries and cultures with precise geographic borders; however it is also synonymous with '1992' and the process of European economic and political unification, presently being carried out under the auspices of that tribute to bureaucracy known as 'The European Community'. My involvement over the past five years in strategy consulting and executive training, both of which have required travel to the far corners of Europe, has exposed me to the confusion and doubts that managers are having in dealing with the issues that surround 'Europe' and has led me to want to take a closer look at what exactly they are doing to demystify the unknown and attempt to pave a smooth path for their respective companies as we near the end of the second millenium.

In attacking the problem, I have opted for a case-study method in the belief that, while theories only give way to more theories, concrete examples may actually give managers, students and politicians alike some specific insight into the challenges and opportunities, as well as the threats, that lie ahead. It must be revealed that the basic premise of this work is the conviction that the future of the developed world's economy lies in an expanded Europe. This having been said, one must inevitably ask, Why? And if so, then what does it imply for managers, regardless of their sectors? What will determine a company's future success or failure? And, more explicitly, what is being done or can be done to safeguard and improve a company's competitive position? It is these issues which I would like to address in this first chapter and which serve as an overview and summary of the results obtained from research conducted in the various companies.

1

THE PROBLEMS

Europe's industrial and economic base is in the midst of confronting problems that are becoming critical in the struggle to guarantee the future of its global competitiveness.

First and foremost is the reluctance of people living in Europe to think of themselves as 'Europeans' rather than French, Portuguese and the like. While most understand the rationale for the process of unification now unfolding, many find it hard to discard the traditional stereotypes characterising other nationalities. This creates tension and an unnecessary waste of human know-how through the duplication of resources (for example, parallel research projects in two or more countries). The Portuguese and Spanish would rather deal with an Englishman or a German than with each other due to age-old political and economic rivalries, yet, for geographic and cultural reasons, they are the most suited to work together. The same applies to the Dutch and the Belgians, the English and the Irish, and so on. This historical lack of co-operation has caused Europe to lose its pre-eminent position in key technological areas such as information systems and electronic equipment and has resulted in an uneven development of the overall infrastructure.

The loss of such a strategic position is further compounded by the American realisation that the future battleground is Europe and not the United States, where the economy is increasingly beset by the problems of deficit spending and unemployment as well as the after-effects of ruthless empire-building based on credit, the likes of which are now being dismantled (as in the case of Donald Trump's empire). This being the case, American managers are changing tactics and following the example of the Japanese by investing heavily in Europe and promoting growth through adaptation rather than acquisition. While this can be considered a positive development, it may catch European managers off-guard.

Looking more deeply into the make-up of Europe's labour force, the prevailing complaint among managers is the lack of available skilled workers as well as the incompatibility of the Community's various national educational systems, making cross-border hiring difficult if not impossible. With schools producing more and more accountants and financiers, there are few affordable technical people left to man the factories. This in turn has caused many companies to employ immigrant workers, a problem in and of itself, as they are apt to be unskilled and their employment tends to create social tension.

Turning more specifically to the European Community (EC) itself, issues become muddled in a bank of rhetorical fog. First and foremost is the fact that, despite its pledge to deregulation and the promotion of maximum industrial efficiency, the EC's policies are actually decreasing the competitiveness of many industries. A large number of Europe's textile companies should have given in to competitive pressures long ago, yet they continue to obtain EC subsidies; many airlines are uncompetitive, yet government subsidies have been rampant (see Chapter 8); national governments still control the transport industry and the import and export of merchandise within EC borders (see Chapter 5).

And then there remain the problems related to the EC's political and judicial process. At present, businesses are trying to gain support for their cause in Brussels, but without knowing who really holds the power. It is not unusual to begin to talk on the telephone in the morning with a member of one of the EC's various divisions, only to be directed to someone else and then again to another person. At the end of the day, one is back to where one started, having accomplished absolutely nothing.

The EC is constantly discussing issues of federalism versus subsidiarity (this states that a national sovereign only delegates upwards that which it cannot do itself). With Italy as the most pro-federalist of the EC nations, and the UK at the other end of the spectrum, the discussions and debates are interminable, creating a situation whereby managers no longer know what they can or cannot do. For instance, the concept of majority vote on EC directives has not been extended to the major fiscal and social issues. Should this change, thus eliminating the power of countries such as the UK and Luxemburg to veto any far-reaching amendments, businesses will find themselves in a dramatically different position, having to revise their entire European employee policies and financial accounting principles. Without a clear idea of the EC's structure, powers and proposed legislation, managers are finding it increasingly difficult to plan on a long-term basis.

THE CHALLENGES

Increasingly beset by corruption, be it intellectual or financial, the European Community and its various member organisations have lost sight of what it is they are striving to achieve and have instead succeeded in building a bureaucracy heretofore unseen in its complexity and inefficiency. While many attribute the reasons for this to such diverse and abstract concepts as human nature and political and economic greed, I believe that it is only the natural result of the increasing divergence between the reality of the business environment and the utopia of the theoreticians and politicians responsible for defining European policy, be it social, legal, business or political.

The central idea behind the creation of a single European market was and remains the creation of an economic space capable of meeting the challenges and threats presented by the leading economic powers; that is, the United States and Japan. In strictly business terminology, the European Community is an attempt to apply, on a massive scale, the logic of economies of scale[1] by providing easy access for commercial enterprises to a potential market of 350 million people, a population larger than either the United States or Japan.

Bearing this in mind, and progressing on the assumption that European economic unification will, in fact, occur, regardless of whether political union follows or not, there are essentially six challenges presently identifiable for the business community as a whole, to be met and overcome in the decade of the 1990s:

1. Because of the Community's inefficiency in adopting and implementing policy, the process of unification and market homogenisation will have to be completed by industrialists and not by politicians.
2. Though 1992 is upon us, barriers to the export and import of research and development, of labour and of financial funds still remain in place. While they are gradually being reduced, the

---

1. Economies of scale imply that the unit costs of production decrease as the cumulative volume of production increases.

new macroeconomic system that looms ahead appears to be deregulated only in name rather than in practice.

3. While 350 million people is a huge potential market, it is not a simple date in history (1 January 1993, for example) that will suddenly and miraculously provide a single consumer market. For the time being, the European Community is still the amalgam of individual countries and cultures, thus providing psychological barriers much more difficult to solve than the existence of legal obstacles.

4. The relatively easy access for all companies to innovative technology as well as the increasing sophistication of the consumer is gradually eroding the traditional competitive advantages such as economies of scale, thus intensifying competition and forcing businesses to seek new ways to compete.

5. Increasing pressure from the consumer is forcing businesses to take a more socially conscious approach to the implementation of their respective strategies.

6. Expanding beyond the borders of Europe, the internationalisation of the world's markets and the tendency towards globalism are undeniable factors in the conduct of business, be it of a multinational or of a domestically-orientated company.

Industrialists will have to Lead the Process of Unification

The year 1992 is considered by many to be the natural end of a process to adapt to the new post-war world order. It is a political process that was initiated in the 1940s on a dual premise: that the fragmentation of the European continent could only be detrimental in its dealings with the emerging superpowers, the Soviet Union and the United States, the latter by far the strongest economic and military power at the time. And that the creation of a supranational organisation which would interlock Europe's economies would, in rational terms, eliminate the risk of another disastrous war.

Today, the idealistic visions which eventually brought about the signing of the Treaty of Rome in 1957 remain in place, but the reality of the world order has changed, outpacing the Brussels machine. The Cold War is theoretically over, thus nullifying fears of another world war, at least with Europe as the battleground; and, above all, the dreamed-of system of interlocking economies has, in fact, installed itself, but on a global scale, without, or perhaps despite, the help of the European Community and other such political organisations. It is no secret that the mere threat of war in the Middle East triggers instantaneous reactions in all the world's major financial markets. With respect to corporate strategies, companies such as Ford have already implemented global production systems, sourcing automobile parts where raw material or labour is cheapest and thus uncoupling production from sales. Italy's industrial magnates Agnelli and De Benedetti have constructed financial empires with holdings that extend throughout the world and which have the potential of controlling entire economies, a situation brought to light during De Benedetti's failed attempt to gain a majority share of Belgium's Générale de Banque.

While Europe's politicians have spent decades discussing and arguing about the relationship between Europe's sovereign governments and the Community's various political, financial and legal institutions, and the amount of power that the former should relinquish to the latter, the world's multinationals spent the decade of the 1970s implementing strategies whose objectives were to circumvent all the barriers to trade that existed throughout the world. The advance in travel technology and the increase in the world's consumer buying power that have been witnessed since the 1950s made such an outlook a prerogative and nowhere has this process been more blatant than in Europe itself. Every country within Europe has, on its own, a relatively small potential market, thus forcing medium-sized and large companies to scan the markets immediately adjoining their own.

Today, the economic need to seek new markets and establish a presence beyond one's own borders has escalated, yet Brussels lags in its adaptation to the new reality. Britain has joined the European Monetary System (EMS), but continues to block any significant legal jurisdiction of the Community within the United Kingdom, particularly when concerning such areas as industrial policy and social laws. Germany is stalling, unable to reconcile its European objectives with its internal unification process. France is eager to see 1992 come to pass, but remains fearful of the relative power of its historical rival Germany, and so on. But rather than consolidate the process already under way and attempt to create a truly supranational structure with its own identity and culture, Brussels is already worrying about whom should be admitted next. Nations from

Sweden to Turkey to Morocco are clamouring to join the Community, lest they suddenly find themselves without an entry into Europe's consumer base.

Bearing in mind the accelerated pace of international economic development and the corresponding lack of progress within the European Community to establish clear competitive frameworks, many companies have taken it upon themselves to implement the policy of economic unification initiated by the politicians, by taking advantage of existing loopholes in Community directives and subsequently presenting Brussels with *faits accomplis*: France's Carnaud became Europe's leading packaging conglomerate when it merged with Britain's Metal Box, thus gaining access to much needed technological innovation (see Chapter 2); SAS Scandinavian Airlines is facing up to European competition by forming strategic alliances with non-Community carriers as well as by exerting significant pressure in Brussels to accelerate the process of industry deregulation (see Chapter 8); the truck manufacturing industry is characterised by complicated patterns of cross-ownership involving companies from every major European country (see Chapter 4).

It is this pressure, exerted by managers with clear visions of where their company and their industry are heading, that will ultimately force Community politicians to reduce the rhetoric and turn to concrete, well defined action.

Overcoming Barriers

The Community's Second Banking Directive allows for a financial institution licensed in one member country to operate throughout the EC, yet this directive does not distinguish between licensing and operating policy, thus allowing for a certain freedom of interpretation by member states. In attempting to deregulate the air travel industry, the EC is actually increasing barriers to competition by its effort to control landing slots and route assignments (see Chapter 8); research and development exchange, perhaps the most important benefit of an open market, is still impeded by national 'non-technical' barriers such as the application of national security clauses or, more commonly, unreasonable certification criteria (for example, the export of a French techno-logy-intensive product to Italy may require the inspection of the company's factory by an Italian official, yet that official may not be available for two or more years).

It is these type of barriers that are dramatically reducing the efficiency of European businesses; as one barrier comes down in Brussels, another just as soon comes into place in the concerned member countries. While methods are being found to circumvent these situations, either based on corporate networking or loose interpretations of Community laws, their future remains uncertain as long as the competition laws are not only clarified, but enforced.

Finding a Common Culture

Many view one of the largest obstacles contributing to corporate inefficiency as being the fragmented nature of Europe's cultural profile. The pervasive application of stereotypical adjectives such as French chauvinism, German efficiency, Italian chaos and British indifference still resound through the halls of Europe's major international corporations and can even be described as being on the rise, in part as a defence mechanism against the fears of giving in to the creation of a 'culture-less' society.

However, it is important to stress that the creation of a common European culture does not imply that all of Europe will soon be speaking the same language, keeping the same hours or laughing at the same jokes. These differences are, in fact, an asset that should be maintained, and even strengthened and put to use in a positive form, promoting the exchange of information, technology and innovation. Each country has, generally speaking, a key success factor of its own, whether it be Italian design ability or French culinary expertise, but none of them are strong enough to compete on their own in the world's present economy.

What a common European culture does signify is the adoption of a common, long-term vision with clear policies and an emphasis on maximising the strengths of each member state. To do so will involve well-thought-out corporate strategies and governmental macroeconomic and industrial policies. The former will, in turn, require balanced training programmes, European-wide communication projects and a uniformity of quality as well as financial incentives. With respect to government and Community actions, the emphasis should be on facilitating the free movement of labour, funds and technology.

Finding New Competitive Advantages

It is estimated that by the year 2000, one half of today's existing companies will have disappeared and that half of the products in use will be totally new. Should this prove to be true, it necessarily implies that the 1990s will be a decade of moving into the unknown. Add to this the widespread availability of technology (one need only look to the proliferation of computer manufacturing and assembling companies in the world) and it becomes apparent that the competitive advantages that have been the cornerstone of corporate strategies in decades past no longer apply.[2]

Economies of scale are now being acquired through mergers and acquisitions, as are the effects of the learning curve. Price differentials are decreasing through the effects of global marketing strategies and increased consumer travel. Distribution channels are simplifying. But if these factors are all disappearing or changing, then the issue becomes one of identifying new ways to compete.

Learning from the Japanese and their global success in industries ranging from motor vehicles to high-tech electronics to hi-fi systems, and based on research in numerous European companies as well as with leading academics, it is widely held that the future success of companies will depend on their ability to use their available technology to promote quality, design and originality. More specifically, such an approach translates into a seemingly contradictory objective of increasing production speed and efficiency while maintaining adaptibility.

On the one hand, this implies improving internal logistics, solidifying and consolidating brand image, centralising research and development and promoting innovation on a Europe-wide and global basis. On the other hand, it means having clearly-defined country strategies, recognising cultural diversity, emphasising national sales, service and distribution plans and, ultimately, customising products.

---

2.   Speech entitled 'Corporate Growth Strategies in the Europe of the 90s', presented by Sir John Harvey-Jones, Chairman, The Economist Group, at the Eurogrowth conference held in London in October 1990.

Mergers and Acquisitions in Europe

The widespread availability of technology has caused many companies to solidify their position via mergers and acquisitions, as indicated by the following figures:[3] in metals and plastics, 24 European companies have merged into 5 since 1985; in white goods, 22 companies have become 9 during the same period; in coffee, 20 companies have become 3, none of which are within the EC; and in the chemical industry, 650 companies have been taken over in a period of six years. Furthermore, with industry concentration levels in Europe well below the levels in the United States, it would appear that there is room for many more such mergers and acquisitions.

However, many barriers to such operations still exist in Europe, among which the fact that 46 per cent of Europe's top 400 companies are not listed on stock exchanges. Those that are listed are spread over fifty different exchanges, compared to the United States' eight. Additionally, EC Directives on mergers and acquisitions, as well as their geographic reach, remain unclear. For example, it would not have occured to most people that the EC could block the acquisition of a Swedish company by a Swiss one (neither of which are in the EC), citing anti-trust reasons, as happened in the case of Tetra-Pak and Alfa-Laval.

Meeting the Social Needs

Taking into the consideration the prospect of restructured and more concentrated industries as well as entirely new products by the year 2000, it seems appropriate to say that the skills available today are not adequate to meet those future needs, be they managerial or

3. Waldenstrom, 'Remaking the Industrial Map of Europe: the Long-Term Implications of EC '92', *Journal for Corporate Growth,* vol. 7 (Deerfield, Ill.: American Association for Corporate Growth, Winter 1991).

technical. Such a problem is further compounded by the fact that the world's higher educational systems presently base their academic programmes on past needs within the professional communities. A majority of the Europe's business schools are still turning out financial experts, accountants, marketing specialists and the like, but few are concentrating on creating the proverbial 'generalist' with a vision that scans an entire industry as opposed to a specific department. In many countries, for example, France, Germany or the Netherlands, students are even required to choose a specific domain during their secondary education, thus further limiting possible experience in adjoining areas.

In an effort to ensure companies' own survival by having the necessary qualified personnel to support the new infrastructures presently being put into place, the challenge for managers in the years to come will be to reach an accord with both the public sector and the individual education systems, to design academic programmes that will meet their respective needs. It is as much a question of self-preservation as civic duty.

The Trend Towards Globalism

One of the most destabilising forces presently at work in the world's businesses is the trend towards widespread internationalisation and globalisation.

At once desired and feared, the process of the internationalisation of the world's markets causes discontinuity and hence uncertainty on both a daily and a long-term basis. While internationalisation may be desired for its expanded market opportunities and increased market homogenisation resulting from widespread travel and the infiltration of supranational consumer habits such as fast food, it also brings headaches in the form of new and untested competition, more demanding and more knowledgeable consumers, and new cultural barriers to overcome. It also signifies the impracticability of significant differences in country strategies (for example, it is almost impossible to apply one price for a product in France and another price in Italy without causing illegal parallel imports as well as consumer confusion and anger). These problems have been further heightened by the installation of cable television, thus transmitting stations across borders.

The challenges presented above apply not only to multinationals, but also, and more emphatically, to domestic enterprises. While the former have a history and corporate philosophy of confronting such issues as internationalisation, social responsibility and political lobbying, the latter have remained relatively protected over the years. Often operating in protected sectors (see Chapter 11), these companies have suffered from a narrow view of their potential markets and have failed to see the rising tide of deregulation accompanied by increased international competition from well-established multinationals. It is the resolution of the problems initially mentioned and the subsequent challenges detailed above that have caused most of Europe's corporate managers to seek innovative solutions.

THE SOLUTIONS

Before turning to the solutions being adopted by European managers in their quest to safeguard their companies' future positions, it is worthwhile looking briefly at the reasons behind the success of the Japanese.

'Japan Inc.' has succeeded in dominating 'high-tech' as well as computer industries and is rapidly gaining in the motor vehicle production sector, despite import quotas in both the United States and Europe. As competition increases, so do the lobbies to stop or at least limit further penetration of the Japanese into the various European markets. However, with the loopholes in Community legislation, such efforts are bound to fail. Citing only one example, Honda has successfully gained a strong foothold by creating joint production and design facilities with Rover in the UK. Hence, the better solution is undoubtedly to try to beat them at their own game. But how?

The Japanese are not known for product innovation as much as they are for product adaptation. Computer technology began in the United States; Philips of Holland created compact-disc technology; the Americans and the Europeans have both been in the motor vehicle industry since the beginning. The secret of the Japanese has been to take the available technology and then improve it according to the specifications of the almighty consumer. Japanese cars offer as standard features that are expensive options on European and

American models; Sony perfected compact-disc technology by offering smaller and less expensive versions, and so on.

In addition to a consumer-driven approach to the market, the Japanese have benefited from their focus on internal development and growth as opposed to profit maximisation, so characteristic of Western companies. Such a perspective has allowed Japanese managers to adopt a longer-term vision, and this has served as justification for high initial investments to gain the needed market share with which subsequently to take advantage of economies of scale. For example, when pricing a new product, the Japanese price not according to costs, but according to the predicted potential market share. This in turn allows for a competitive retail price from the very beginning and actually accelerates the gain of market share and the corresponding cost savings associated with the economies of scale.

On the production side, the true innovation in Japan has come with the creation of 'just-in-time' production systems, thereby minimising stock levels, as well as with highly flexible computerised production lines capable of switching rapidly from one product to another.[4] At the heart of these systems lies an extremely complex network of small firms supplying, on an exclusive basis, the larger multinationals. However, equally important has been the emphasis on 'zero-defect' products, implemented through total quality control programmes, in an effort to win consumer respect.

While the above is but a rapid overview and does not attempt to go into great detail – nor does it go into the effects of the gradual infiltration of Western social and cultural values into Japanese society,[5] it does give an idea of areas to be perfected in Europe.

---

4. 'Just-In-Time' implies that the necessary materials for production are supplied only as they are needed, as opposed to being bought and then stored. This has been facilitated by the practice of extensive subcontracting to exclusive suppliers.
5. In Japan, an employee is considered an employee for life and his company forms an integral part of his social and personal life. However, the increased exposure to European and American values and culture is changing this, causing a greater desire for self-fulfilment and individuality. Companies are encountering more and more difficulty in attracting employees and in obtaining loyalty to the same extent as in the past.

The ultimate goal of Europe's business community is to increase efficiency and quality so as to be able to compete on equal terms with non-EC multinational and global corporations. In order to do so, there are essentially four alternatives that managers are opting for:

- mergers and acquisitions
- globalism
- networking
- sustainable niche strategies.

Mergers and Acquisitions

Mergers and acquisitions have been among the headlines of business journals and newspapers since the 1970s, when the concept became a fad. But in contrast to the 1970s and 1980s, when the objective of such mergers and acquisitions was to diversify into any and all areas, provided they were potentially profitable, managers today view such a strategic move as a means to gain the necessary critical volume within a well defined industry as well as to gain access to research and development (see Chapter 2).

Most mergers and acquisitions are seen as a high risk alternative because of their historically worrying failure rate. While the reasons for such failures have ranged from diversification into areas unfamiliar to the managers in question to the incompatibility of management styles and corporate philosophies, today the problems in such European ventures have tended to be related to cultural/nationality differences. Yet it is precisely these differences that in many instances can be the key success factor. Provided the management is able to bridge the gap between nationalities by creating a totally new, and overriding, corporate culture, a European merger or acquisition provides an opportunity to maximise the positive elements of the different groups. As in the case of CMB (Chapter 2), a French multinational with a strong market presence merged with its British counterpart, thereby acquiring access to research and development and marketing expertise. So as to overcome cultural barriers between the French and the British employees, heavy emphasis was placed on extensive internal communications and the creation of a totally new corporate operating procedure. In the process, the new CMB Packaging became the leading packaging conglomerate in Europe, thus gaining the critical volume needed to take advantage of economies of scale. Symbolic of the 1990s approach towards mergers and acquisitions, CMB discarded any and all areas unrelated to the core business, whether they were profitable or not.

Globalism

'Globalism' is the catchword of the 1990s, and refers to a company's ability to take advantage of global market opportunities. As a point of clarification, a multinational differs from a global corporation in that the former considers opportunities on a 'country market' basis. With the increased costs associated with multinational management, the concept of globalism is rapidly gaining strength particularly in Europe, and has potentially far-reaching effects on the future of corporate management.

Multinational management implies creating independent management structures in each operating country. Marketing, production and sales decisions are made at the local level by managers working with a centrally-administered budget. As a rule, they remain quite free to implement their strategies, provided these fall within the overall corporate guidelines as communicated from headquarters.

Turning specifically to Europe, it has become increasingly apparent that such an approach is not often workable, if for no other reason than the sheer number of different countries involved. However, the problems are not only related to managerial costs. Operating in what is a relatively concentrated geographic market, duplication of effort has become rampant. For instance, a marketing team in The Netherlands will be doing the same job at the same cost as a marketing team in Germany, yet for markets of a vastly different size. Reduce this to a cost per individual and then multiply it by the number of countries and one immediately sees the waste in resources. Such a waste is often further heightened by a lack of communication between the various operating units, thus causing parallel research projects and product innovations across different geographic areas.

Looking at this with respect to the market, the risk of creating customer confusion is high. Because of the autonomy of multinational operating units, nothing says that a strategy in Italy will be the same as one in Germany. Should this be the case, the consumer, who travels more and more, could become confused at the inconsistencies in product and brand strategies and could eventually reject the product.

Unlike multinationalism, globalism implies a centralisation of authority at headquarters: in an effort to create a coherent global image and to reduce costs related to production, sales and marketing, some or all decisions are made centrally and then communicated to the various profit units whose role it is to implement, adapting to local conditions only when necessary. Global structures tend to be lighter and more flexible than multinationals precisely because the ultimate authority is centralised, thus reducing the chains of communication. However, there are three problems immediately identifiable with such an approach.

First, the transition from a multinational to a global company risks creating a conflictual relationship between senior and middle managers (see Chapter 8), as the latter suddenly find themselves with little or no decision-making power. The resolution of this problem requires a redefinition of the role of middle managers, putting greater emphasis on market research, vertical communication and training for lower-level managers.

Secondly, despite trends towards a universal consumer, cultural differences still remain. Bearing this in mind, it remains difficult to appeal to, for example, a Danish consumer with the same arguments one would use in Spain. In an effort to overcome this obstacle, more and more companies are resorting to brand and institutional as opposed to product-specific advertising. This approach subsequently allows greater flexibility of adaptation with respect to the latter as well as reduced costs.

Thirdly, the differences in internal infrastructures and distribution systems across Europe are still great and can therefore require country specific adaptation of global distribution strategies. This problem will only be resolved with time and investment.

Networking

Networking is undoubtedly the option being put into practice on the widest scale. Simply put, networking implies the creation of strategic alliances with national and international competitors in an effort mutually to reduce costs by pooling resources and promoting the exchange of know-how, market expertise, sales expertise, and so on.

Greatly used by smaller companies which do not have the ability to compete with their larger counterparts, networking has the advantage of decreasing costs, providing time gains, decreasing risks, increasing one's relative economic power and decreasing barriers to future development (see Chapters 4, 5 and 8).

Such strategies have been the backbone of Germany's medium sized companies as well as of Japan's major industries, and have the distinct advantage of avoiding the high risks associated with mergers and acquisitions.

What is essential to guarantee the success of networking is that the two or more parties have a clear vision of their respective object-ives and what it is they hope to gain from one another. The moment such an agreement is viewed as being too beneficial for one member to the detriment of the other(s), the system is apt to break down.

Sustainable Niche Strategies

Finally, for those companies fearful of competing with larger international competitors because of a lack of resources, but also unwilling or unable to find networking candidates, there remains the possibility of seeking out and focusing exclusively on specific market segments. Because of their limited potential, such segments are often unprofitable for larger competitors to devote much time or resources to, and they can therefore provide a steady source of income. However, such an approach does not make the company immune from an eventual hostile take-over bid, a phenomenon on the rise as the European markets open up to each other.

Which alternative a company chooses will ultimately depend on its long-term objectives as well as the type of product made. If one has the potential and the desire to be a major European actor, then the route to achieve such a goal is undoubtedly through well planned and coherent mergers or acquisitions whose objective it is to accumulate market share. The success of such a choice will be a function of a management's ability to oversee the integration of diverse corporate and national cultures and of the ability to turn down options simply because they present profit potential. Whether or not to go global can only be based on whether the benefits (that is, cost reductions through lower overheads and uniform, coherent

Co-operation from the perspective of German and Italian managers[6] – an overview:

Germany

While the preoccupation of the German government is, and will continue to be in the foreseeable future, the integration of East Germany into the economic and social system of the Federal Republic, managers remain with their sights on international markets, including the European Community.

For obvious geographic reasons, historically German managers have adopted an export mentality, with particular emphasis given to Austria and Switzerland because of the common language, and have thus always been conscious of providing products suitable to the different needs of the various countries.

Thus far, German companies have, by and large, met with success within Europe as their products are universally recognised for their superior quality. This being the case, the need for co-operation on a technological basis has never been high.

However, studies reveal that German managers are open to specific proposals of foreign co-operation, particularly in the area of competitor analysis, a domain requiring in-depth knowledge of domestic markets.

Italy

Northern Italy, the heartbeat of Italy's industry, has witnessed a dramatic boom in its overall economic wealth during the decade of the 1980s. At the root of the competitive policies adopted by the leading industrial empires, such as Gianni Agnelli's Fiat or Silvio Berlusconi's Fininvest, as well as those of the small and medium-sized family-run companies, has

---

6. The information provided in this highlight is based on the author's exchanges with managers while conducting market research, as well as information obtained from studies whose results are published in P. Joffre and G. Koenig, *L'Euro-entreprise* (Paris: Economica, 1989).

been an aggressive approach towards the European market. Realising that the Italian consumer base is geographically concentrated and relatively limited in size, these companies have purposely built excess production capacity with the sole aim of competing in the neighbouring markets of France, Switzerland, Germany, Austria and Eastern Europe. The basis of this competition lies in the Italians' reputation for quality products with a distinct design.

This having been said, Italian managers believe that co-operation of any kind can only be a commercial asset when attempting to penetrate foreign markets. With respect to technology, Italian companies have thus far favoured co-operation agreements with the United States, Japan and Germany (see Chapters 3 and 5).

---

strategies) outweigh the losses (that is, possible loss of middle managers, or loss of certain specific segments due to the application of a generic strategy).

If, on the other hand, being number one is not the aim, then networking allows for maximum autonomy while taking advantage of know-how and information exchange to mutually strengthen each company's position.

CONCLUSION

The initial premise of this book and, specifically this chapter, has been that Europe will be the corporate battleground of the future, yet the mere fact of having a population base larger than that of the United States is not enough to justify such a statement.

The reasons for such a conviction lie instead in the intellectual, technological and cultural diversity that characterise Europe, but that have never really been put to use in a concerted and positive manner. Even without the elimination of political, economic and industrial barriers, Europe already boasts many of the world's leading corporations and technological innovations: with respect to companies, one need only mention Philips, Daimler-Benz, Airbus Industrie, Fiat, among many others to realise that the access to financial and intellectual resources is tremendous. Turning to technological innovations, the banking sector is, for example, far in advance of the American equivalent when it comes to meeting the needs of its clients across regions and across borders (for example, while it is possible to cash a Eurocheque or withdraw money via automatic tellers in most of Europe, it is still difficult to use a New York cheque outside the state of New York).

On the assumption that such energy and efforts can be channelled in a constructive form, through co-operation and exchange on both a micro- and a macroeconomic level, then it seems apparent that the necessary elements to compete globally do exist. This said, competing in the Europe of the 1990s is providing managers with two simultaneous and contradictory objectives: increased efficiency combined with heightened market responsiveness. The former carries with it a need for central co-ordination, while the latter asks for decentralisation and a more personalised approach to the needs of the consumer.

The creation of a single economic market is putting managers in touch with previously unknown competitors and, as a result, is exerting pressure to increase the pace of innovation as well as the variety of products offered to an ever more demanding consumer.

While it seems certain that this process of market unification will cause the exit of many companies unwilling or unable to compete in

---

Redefining Europe's Economy[7]

While the focus of the case studies presented in this book is on individual company response to the challenges of the 1990s in Europe, it is important to note that a certain emphasis has been placed on the service sector, if only to reflect the changes taking place in the overall structure of Europe's economy: between 1978 and 1988, the industrial sector declined from 32 per cent to 28.2 per cent and agriculture from 5 per cent to 4.4 per cent, while services rose from 63 per cent to 67.4 per cent of total GNP.

---

7. Panorama of EC Industry (Brussels: EC Industrial Economic Services, 1990).

the new competitive environment, as well as the streamlining of existing corporations through more efficient factories (for example, by the installation of multi-purpose machines), more emphasis on computer-aided design and manufacturing, and a greater effort to promote networking, it is equally certain that the long-term benefits will come in the form of more productive economies, more consumer satisfaction and, with increased co-operation between the public and private sectors, better qualified personnel.

The Macroeconomic Benefits of European Unification[8]

To give an indication of the waste resulting at present from duplication of effort and from unnecessary bureaucracy, the figures below have been calculated to estimate the cost of a 'non-Europe':

Potential GNP gains, in billions of ECUs (European Currency Units), resulting from

The elimination of trade barriers	8–9
The elimination of technological barriers	57–71
Gains from economies of scale	61
Benefits from increased competition	46
Total	174–258

or roughly equal to 4.3–6.4 per cent of Europe's actual GNP. From the perspective of costs, the present European system causes:

- 7500 million ECUs in administrative expenses;
- between 415 and 830 million ECUs in delays;
- between 4500 and 15000 million ECUs in lost business; and
- between 500 and 1000 million ECUs in border control expenses.

---

8. P. Cecchini, *1992 – The European Challenge* (London: Wildwood House, 1989).

Part I
European Industry

2 CMB Packaging: Dissecting a Transnational Merger

As 1992 approaches, many managers are experiencing a rude awakening to the insecurities of deregulation and the risk of foreign incursions into their own markets, space once thought inviolable. They are being caught off-guard and embarking on a frantic race to secure their positions once again through *ad hoc* joint ventures, mergers or acquisitions. Potential partners are sought out, approached and, 'under the sword of Damocles', contracts are signed; yet they fail to realise that their respective initiatives may be doomed from the start. While the new market share figures may suddenly have boosted their companies to unimagined heights, the 'soft' or cultural aspects of the deal are often ignored and devalued. This is particularly true in instances of cross-cultural mergers or acquisitions. While joining up two companies, whatever the legal form may be, is already a complicated matter, transnational deals face even greater obstacles. The problems are no longer limited to reconciling different corporate cultures, but extend to communication barriers, issues of national pride and questions of logistics, such as on whose home turf headquarters should be located.

CMB's Chairman, French-born Jean-Marie Descarpentries, has been dealing with these issues constantly since 1989, when French Carnaud merged with British Metal Box to create one of the world's leading packaging conglomerates whose aim it is to be number one in its field in Europe and, with time, number one in the world too. His methods have created controversy on both sides of the Channel, with the English perhaps all too eager to declare the merger a failure, and the French a little hasty in calling it a success. For the English, Descarpentries has succeeded in sequestering one of their jewels of industry, turning it into a 'European', or yet worse, a French entity, while for the French, it is an example of the new European spirit permeating the air throughout the continent.

In truth, neither are correct, being misguided by their sense of national pride; it is far too early to pass such a definitive verdict. The issue, at this stage, should not be whether the merger is a success or a failure, but instead an evaluation of the rationale for and the obstacles to such a venture. Everyone speaks of the 'new Europe', but with little understanding of what this means, particularly in a corporate context. What does it imply to turn a company into a European leader? How does one define 'leader'? How does one implement such a strategy? Can the cultural barriers really be overcome?

LOOKING TO MERGE

The European packaging industry is characterised by extreme fragmentation: today, the top ten groups account for only 22.5 per cent of the European market, estimated at 450 billion French francs,[1] of which CMB has an estimated 5 per cent. Going back to the early 1980s, this situation was even more acute. Made up almost entirely of small and medium-sized companies, the remaining packaging conglomerates such as French Pechiney, BSN, Saint Gobain and Carnaud, American Continental Can and British Metal Box slept. They and their industry crept along, hardly responding to the needs of the market despite the major changes taking place since the consumer boom of the 1960s.

With the consumer boom, large scale distribution came into being and advertising began its rapid ascent to the omnipresent and ever powerful status we now witness in the 1990s. The consumer developed new habits: women went to work, disposable income increased, cooking habits changed – in short, convenience became the order of the day. Packaging not only had to serve a functional purpose (that is, to preserve freshness, for ease of storage, ease of handling, and so on), but it also had to seduce the consumer. Yet, despite these signals, the leading packaging houses stagnated; they entered a boom market unprepared.

---

1. This figure includes the Eastern European market. Excluding Eastern European countries, the market is estimated at 350 billion French francs.

In 1982, the French Carnaud lagged behind its main competitors. With accumulated losses totalling 63 million French francs, Carnaud lacked technological leadership as well as an aggressive mentality and a clear cut strategy for the future, as symbolised by its 'stock' mentality: Carnaud had twice the level of stock needed, but its managers found it difficult to get out of this syndrome and thus the problem seemed to grow only worse. It was, in fact, an ideal candidate for a take-over and many thought Metal Box would jump in.[2]

Metal Box, the star of the British packaging industry, was known to have a strong research and development department as well as a capable marketing staff, yet it was unable to solidify its market position, due primarily to its centralised structure. While the various divisions were solid, there was no cross-communication and the innovations introduced remained unresponsive to market needs. Furthermore, it is felt that Metal Box's management did not fully believe in their mission and they lacked a vision of the future Europe. They failed to seize the opportunity of gaining a foothold in the continental European market – this lack of foresight was to come back and haunt them only a few years later.

Enter Jean-Marie Descarpentries as Chairman of Carnaud Emballage and subsequently Chairman of Carnaud S.A. A Harvard graduate, Descarpentries has raised eyebrows because of his draconian management policies, but has gained praise for his ability to turn companies around. Applying concepts and techniques learned during his stay at Shell and then McKinsey, the American management consulting group, Descarpentries brought to life a failing Belgian subsidiary of the French group BSN as well as a Spanish subsidiary of the group St. Gobain. Hence not unfamiliar with the packaging industry, Descarpentries moved on to devote himself to Carnaud. By imposing a new, completely decentralised structure and reducing staff by over 3500 employees (without having to actually fire anyone), Carnaud was on the road to profit within two years. However, restructuring was only the beginning. What was needed was a clearly thought out strategy to consolidate and strengthen the group's position in France and the world.

---

2. Carnaud was a licensee of Metal Box at the time.

Despite a return to profitability, Carnaud still lacked technological leadership and also risked spreading itself too thinly across different businesses. Descarpentries, stating a corporate mission, defined the group's business as packaging and metal and plastics closures, and subsequently began a second phase of house-cleaning. Any and all businesses which did not fit into the scheme of packaging were sold, as was the case with its steel operations, which were relinquished to Pechiney, even though this division had a good reputation and was profitable.

Personnel productivity increased through the acquisition of state-of-the-art machinery and heavy investments in personnel training, as well as the introduction of an employee profit-sharing scheme. Gradually, not only the structure of the group changed, but also the way of thinking. The changes begun in the old Carnaud were to be continued and perfected well into the early 1990s, after the merger with Metal Box.

House-cleaning was not, however, Descarpentries' only objective. Having succeeded in making Carnaud a new force in the French packaging industry, he wanted to move on and secure the company's position on a global level. Descarpentries is a man who believes that the future belongs to those who have reached the critical size factor necessary to call the shots in the marketplace and have significant economies of scale, primarily in research and development and marketing. The future belongs to those who have the clout to control their cost of capital and to those who remain flexible enough so as to be able to take calculated risks on opportunities as they present themselves. Reaching a size where this is possible can be achieved either through internal development or acquisitions or both. Convinced that time was of the essence, Descarpentries opted for both alternatives, but with a definite preference for acquisitions. Eager to ascertain Carnaud's new role in European industry, its management began the search for a merger partner.

Ideally, a merger partner will complement your own company in every way, from corporate culture to clients to production techniques. Yet, in reality, the result of the search is often a function of which company is willing to talk at the same time as you are. Descarpentries and his staff scanned the potential list of partners and, paradoxically, found themselves at the negotiating table with Metal Box, only this time with the roles reversed. While Metal Box had continued to stagnate, Carnaud was now negotiating from a position of strength. In April 1988 the creation of CMB Packaging was announced.

THE MERGER

The logic of the annouced merger lay in the idea that Carnaud and Metal Box complemented each other: Metal Box had a strong informations system, a strong marketing department and strong research and development. On the other hand, Carnaud was in a healthier position relative to competition, both in terms of its balance sheet and its market share. Furthermore, Carnaud had a vision of Europe, an outlook definitely lacking on the other side of the Channel. How much of this reasoning was developed after the fact, however, remains unknown.

With the creation of CMB Packaging, an elated Chairman promised to have his company leading the world packaging industry. With a combined staff of 33 000 people, a presence in over fifteen countries and one of the most aggressive strategies in the industry, Descarpentries promised higher returns and a European market share of 10 per cent or more by 1992. In early 1991, CMB's market share stood at a little under 5 per cent and the financial results lagged behind predictions: restructuring costs had come in higher than expected, finance charges had increased and the stock value in the UK had gone down. For a man who believes the only worthwhile means of measurement are numbers, things were not looking good. Even worse, predictions for 1991 put the ambitions of 1988 yet a little further out of reach. Perhaps because of Descarpentries' extravagant and outspoken style, the press took a hard line, particularly in Britain. However, taking into consideration the magnitude of the changes realised within the company, it is surprising the results were not worse.

'MAXIMUM DECENTRALISATION, MAXIMUM COHESION'

Turning a company around and bringing it to the forefront of its industry requires, in most cases, a change of mentality. In

companies that have stagnated, the employees are often characterised by poor motivation and low productivity as well as a certain
sense of fatalism with respect to the future, and mistrust towards the
senior management. They have heard promises of roads paved with
gold only just around the corner, yet the corner always appears to
be a little out of reach, and so they become disgruntled. This may be
particularly true of companies operating in France and other Latin
countries, where the historical tendency has been for the supposedly
omniscient managers to hold a tight rein on all the employees. The
only ones with the power and the knowledge to decide have been
those at the top. Yet, as SAS Scandinavian Airlines' President, Jan
Carlzon, has often stated, the complexity of today's economy and
competition has undermined the capacity of even the best manager.
It is virtually impossible for a single individual to have the full
knowledge necessary for all decision-making. That being the case,
what is the role of the new manager and how does one change the
employees' way of thinking and thus reinstate motivation and
personal initiative?

Descarpentries, upon joining Carnaud, identified one major
problem as being the bottlenecking of decisions at the top. The
senior management was too far removed from the market and,
furthermore, had grown lazy. The rift between the senior staff and
the employees was rapidly heading towards being an unbridgeable
chasm. A drastic measure was needed, which came in the way of the
'inverted pyramid'.

The inverted pyramid corresponds more to a new way of thinking
rather than a specific structure, but is, however, an essential step
towards facilitating the realisation of the new organisation chart
chosen. The idea behind the pyramid is that the client, and not the
senior executive officer, is at the top of the ladder. Senior management subsequently moves down to a 'behind the scenes' role
situated at the bottom, with the shareholders. However, based on
the concept of the classic pyramid, the operational decisions are still
made at the top. Then if the senior management is at the bottom,
who is making the decisions? The employees closest to the client are.
Overall a relatively simple concept, though with a far reaching
implication: the order-taker suddenly turns into a decision maker.
While he could get by in the past by delegating decision-making
upwards, he no longer can. But from a practical standpoint, how
does one implement such a structure?

The inverted pyramid concept was introduced to Carnaud in the early 1980s, thus prior to the creation of CMB Packaging. In an effort to decentralise, the company was divided into various business units, comprised of three categories: 'departments' for business units with a turnover of 0–100 million French francs, 'divisions' for a turnover between 100 and 500 million French francs; and, finally, 'entities' for those units with a turnover greater than 500 million French francs. The creation of these business units put managers in the front line, in direct contact with the customer and directly responsible for year-end results. Today, within CMB Packaging, there exist a total of 100 business units.

However, the creation in and of itself of business units is not enough. Accompanying such a structure further implies new internal mechanisms of evaluation and communication to help convey to the employees the new corporate philosophy. With respect to internal evaluation mechanisms, each business unit is expected to improve results continuously on a year-to-year basis. To monitor the unit's performance, its results are compared to those of other business units operating in the same sector as well as to those of competing companies and, finally, the unit is measured against itself on an historical basis. The method used to evaluate the performance is based on three indicators, submitted monthly to the senior management: turnover growth rate; working capital requirement/turnover; and net profit. The key to decentralisation is transparency: 'each key figure, one manager'. Furthermore, there is no intervention from senior management should a problem arise within a particular business unit. Instead, the situation is monitored from afar, with the appropriate warning signals issued (that is, indications of poor ratios compared to other business units and competitors).

But such a programme required a well-thought-out internal communications strategy to ensure that all share a common vision of the future and how to get there. Hence, Descarpentries initiated monthly newsletters and began annual meetings of all the company's business unit managers. This policy has continued in CMB Packaging and has been supplemented with international employee ownership plans (presently, more than 10 000 employees participate) as well as stock options for the top 700 managers and common incentive schemes for the top 200 managers.

Carnaud was well on the way to a new way of thinking when the merger with Metal Box was announced, thus creating additional problems. The new Carnaud structure had to be reconciled with, on the one hand, the centralised and hierarchical mentality of Metal Box and, on the other, the age old cultural differences and rivalries that have existed between the French and the English.

With Descarpentries' tendency to be outspoken and heavy-handed, the risk of the British perceiving the merger more as a French 'take-over' was high. They were about to see a new organisation chart imposed on them, but according to French specifications. So as to minimise sentiments of ill-will and rivalry, it was decided that the best solution was to put not just the British or the French on 'enemy territory', but *everyone*. As a first step, the official language of the new CMB Packaging was to be English, though the British were strongly encouraged to perfect their French. Secondly, headquarters would not be either in Paris or London, but in Brussels. and lastly, a culture based on ratios, begun during the Carnaud turnaround, was to be implemented with full force.

Today, CMB operates out of Paris, London and Brussels, the latter being where senior management resides. There are, of course, inconveniences such as extensive travel between the three cities; however, taking into consideration the travel already required of the senior management of a multinational, CMB believes the present structure poses no additional hurdles to the company's efficient operations, particularly as the senior executives' function is no longer to make daily operational decisions, but instead to concentrate on predicting the clients' needs, the personnel's and shareholders' needs and to decide on overall strategy guidelines.

The only function presently centralised is that of recruitment of managers who are seen as having the potential to rise up to senior management positions. Initially interviewed at the business unit level, the candidates must then go through a series of evaluations with members of the senior staff. This ideally has the advantage of avoiding favouritism and the creation of little 'clubs' within the company.

ADJUSTING COURSE

The change in corporate culture initiated in Carnaud during the early 1980s was only just beginning to take root when CMB came into existence in 1989. Yet despite the tremendous challenge that such a merger involved, Descarpentries still aimed for a 10 per cent market share within Europe by 1993; he believes such a strategy is not only possible, but essential to the survival of his company in the long run. After all, not only is the market situation still very fragmented, thus providing innumerable opportunities for acquisitions, but the per capita consumption of packaging in Europe is well below that of the United States and Japan,[3] thus providing room for almost limitless growth in the decade ahead. By mid-1991, with the definition of Europe now extended to include Eastern Europe, and the market estimated at 450 billion French francs as opposed to 350bn, Descarpentries still had the same objective of a 10 per cent market share, though the year was no longer specified. In fact, in 1990, CMB's market share within Europe was estimated at 4–5 per cent and predictions for 1991 were filled more with gloom and apprehension than elated optimism. What, if anything, went wrong?

Descarpentries is perhaps his own worst enemy in that he undermines his reputation among the blood-hungry wolves of the press by being over-enthusiastic. When the results fall short of the promises made to the outside world, the attacks begin and the rumours of yet another failed merger begin to travel. But a merger of this magnitude rarely matures in one or two years.

CMB produces packaging primarily for the agro-food sector (68 per cent of sales), followed by speciality packaging (16 per cent), health and beauty (8 per cent) and aerosols (4 per cent). Within the agro-food sector, 10 per cent is for beverages, 53 per cent for food products and 5 per cent is made up of closures. While the agro-food segment is relatively free from the ups and downs of economic cycles, the others remain very dependent on the overall state of the economy, thus instilling a degree of uncertainty and proportionate risk into CMB's turnover.

Using Descarpentries' own criteria for judging the success or failure of a merger, the numbers for 1990 reflected not only some of this additional risk factor associated with certain market segments,

---

3. Per capita yearly consumption of packaging is estimated at 290 kilos in the United States, 180 kilos in Europe and 5 kilos in developing countries (*Source*: CMB Packaging).

CMB Packaging's Products and Clients

Products

- Aluminium and white iron beverage cans. These products are experiencing a high growth rate due to the ease of use of the can and the growth of the soft-drinks market worldwide.
- Standard and personalised food cans. CMB is European leader and has an important presence in Africa and Australasia.
- Aerosol cans.
- A full line of packaging for the cosmetics and pharmaceutical industries. Through its subsidiaries AMS in France and Risdon in the United States, CMB is world leader in this segment.
- High-performance plastics, for example for use in microwave ovens.
- Specialised, multi-layered packaging using, for example, plastic and aluminium.

Clients

CMB Packaging counts among its client base the world's leading consumer-goods manufacturers: Coca Cola; Mars Group; Nestlé; Unilever; Bass/Britvic; Heinz; Schweppes; Procter & Gamble; Hillsdown; BSN; Pepsi-Cola; Bonduelle; Cecab; Quaker; L'Oréal. Together, these fifteen companies made up 32 per cent of CMB's total turnover in 1990, compared to 28 per cent in 1989.

but also extra costs unpredicted at the time of the merger (see Tables 2.1, 2.2, 2.3 and 2.4).

Heading the list of unexpected costs were astronomical restructuring expenses to the order of 617 million French francs, together with large finance charges associated not only with the restructuring, but also with the acquisition of numerous companies, primarily in Europe.

Table 2.1   CMB Packaging: overall performance figures (in millions of French francs)

	1986	1987	1988	1989	1990
Total turnover (billions)	6.6	7.2	9.4	24.1	24.4
Finance charges	–	–	–	(647)	(726)
Total sales less cost of goods sold	478	537	792	2 007	2 219
Gross profit*	–	–	–	1 649	1 607
Net profit after taxes	217	365	527	1 195	1 028

Notes:
* Gross profit is calculated as total turnover less cost of goods sold, depreciation and finance charges.

Table 2.2   CMB Packaging: key ratios and indicators

Indicators	1986	1987	1988	1989	1990
Total staff	–	–	–	36 616	33 948
Total investments (in millions of Ffr)	665	1 108	1 263	2 488	2 290
Gross margins as % total sales					
Metals	–	–	–	–	10.5%
Plastics	–	–	–	–	5.5%
Multi-material	–	–	–	–	6.5%
Other	–	–	–	–	5.9%
Group	–	–	–	–	9.1%
Personnel costs/total sales	22.8%	21.7%	20.5%	22.5%	22.4%
Working capital requirement (days)	75	64	62	51	41
Finance charges/total sales	3.1%	2.6%	2.2%	2.7%	3.0%*
Productivity sales/employee** (in thousands of Ffr)	–	740	805	668	719
Dividend/share (Ffr)	1.7	2.1	3	3.6	3.6***

Notes:
* 0.3% due to increase in interest rate.
** In 1981, the sales per employee were 370,000 Ffr.
*** Proposed.

Table 2.3   CMB Packaging: debt structure

	1988	1989	1990
Debt + preferred stock (in millions of Ffr)			6 383
Variable debt* (%)			43
Fixed debt *			57
Currency split (Ffr equivalent)			
British pounds			1 961
French francs			1 443
Italian lire			686
US dollars			613
German marks			506
Spanish pesetas			495
Other			679
Total debt in billions of Ffr	1.3	4.8	2.4**
Total debt/total equity	39%	48%	16%

Notes:
* As of 31 December 1989.
** Reduction due to new issue of preferential stock.

Table 2.4   CMB Packaging: internal growth rates, 1990/1989 (in percentages)

	Percentage total sales	Growth 1990/1989
Metals, agro-food	35	2
Metals, beverage*	10	22
Metals, industrial	10	-2
Bottles, plastic closures	8	4
Health & beauty	8	-3
Metal closures*	5	11
Africa, Middle East	5	1
Asia/Pacific	4	-1
Engineering/technology	4	2
Aerosols	4	-4
Flexible packaging	3	11
High performance plastics	3	7
Composites	1	8

Notes:
* The growth rate indicated is higher than the average industry rate.

CMB's Acquisitions: The Road to being Market Leader

In 1990 alone CMB added almost 1.5 billion French francs to its total turnover by acquiring fifty or so companies. While many of these companies will choose to retain their old identity, slightly modified to include 'CMB Packaging' in the logo, they will now profit from the financial, technological and logistical resources of the entire group. The acquisitions included companies in the following segments:

Product	Segment served	Total sales (millions Ffr)
Metals	Agro-food	98
	Industrial	212
Plastics	Bottles/closures	411
	Health and beauty	49
Multi-material	Flexible packaging	110

In addition, companies representing total sales of 143 million French francs were acquired in Africa and the Asia/Pacific region.

Both Metal Box and Carnaud were fat in staff at the time of the merger, which necessitated a certain amount of 'cleaning out'. In fact, in 1990, CMB registered departures of 12.9 per cent of the total 36 500 employees worldwide, though this was somewhat counter-balanced by the hiring of 2043 new employees in an effort to bring in new blood and expertise to help promote the new culture. A 5.6 per cent recruitment level is extremely high and should eventually settle down at around 1.5 per cent per annum once the company has reached cruising speed.

Furthermore, as we have seen, Metal Box was highly centralised at the time of the merger and therefore had to be divided into separate business units to ensure a streamlined and coherent organisation. While it is easy to conceive of this on paper, in reality it necessitates a reorganisation of the logistics and information systems worldwide as well as investment in management training to help staff deal with the shock of suddenly being responsible for their own bottom-line. Surprisingly, though, the number of departures due to the change in management style at senior levels was limited.

However, the poor results obtained during the first full year of existence of CMB Packaging were due not only to the internal situation, but came about also from a series of 'accidents' reflecting the vulnerability of certain business units to economic downturns as well as the threat of intense competition from Japan.

On the competitive front, CMB faced head-on intense Japanese competition when it tried to enter the Thai fish can and beverage market. While CMB has been able to finally establish itself, it could be a warning for the future should the Japanese enter the European market in full force.

CMB's Competition

While the packaging industry remains fragmented, the world's top twelve packaging corporations accounting for only 16 per cent of the total estimated world market, CMB nevertheless faces some difficult competitors who have recently woken up to the possibilities within their markets and are now eagerly seeking to emulate CMB in its growth strategy.

In 1990, the classification of the top twelve was as follows:

	Estimated 1990 sales (in billions of Ffr)
ANC Pechiney	29.7 (32 in 1989)
Toyo Seikan	32
CMB Packaging	24.4
Tetra-Pak	24
Owens Brockway	19.8
Crown Cork/CC USA	18.5
Sonoco	10.5
Van Leer	9.4
St. Gobain	9.2
Continental Can Eur.	7.3
BSN	5.9
PLM	5.4 (6.1 in 1989)

However, such a table is misleading in that, while all the above are in packaging, the market segments covered by each are quite different.

As an example, Van Leer packaging, a Dutch multinational, characterised by its secrecy, operates mainly in the industrial sector and obtains most of its sales from outside Europe, as does Pechiney. Tetra-Pak, based in Switzerland, is essentially a mono-product company (cardboard milk and juice boxes), though it is attempting to diversify via acquisition.

Looking strictly at the European market, the line-up is slightly different, with the top fifteen companies accounting for approximately 22 per cent of the European market:

CMB Packaging – 21.2 bn Ffr (equal to 87 per cent of
   CMB's total turnover)
Tetra-Pak – 15 bn Ffr
Pechiney –10.7 bn Ffr
Saint Gobain – 8.1 bn Ffr
Continental Can – 7.3 bn Ffr
PLM – 5.4 bn Ffr
BSN – 5.9 bn Ffr

The following all have a European turnover of under 5 billion French francs: Van Leer, Alusuisse, Linpac, Lawson-Mardon Group, Gerresheimer, Crown Cork, Rockware and Nord-Est.

The cosmetics, or health and beauty, segment is subject to a certain degree of instability as its sales are dependent on the overall health of the economy and the subsequent purchasing power of the consumer. In this area, CMB has been experiencing a negative growth rate due to the slowing of the economy and to certain internal organisational problems. In order to alleviate this situation, the CMB management began in 1990 a restructuring of its health and beauty operations so as to be able to increase efficiency and adaptability. Concretely, these changes caused the closure of one factory, the addition of state-of-the-art equipment and the division of the various business units' structure along three major sub-segments: pharmaceuticals, health, and perfume/make-up. One factory has been completely converted to the production of only pharmaceutical packaging products and is the only one in the world to produce the packaging and the closures under the same roof.

Additional 'accidents' have included the loss of market share due to strikes in the United Kingdom.

Turning more specifically to the internal problems, CMB still carries the weight of poor efficiency levels and high working capital requirements. While the working capital requirements are decreasing, it is still as high as 200 days in some business units,

With respect to efficiency, CMB factories have improved due to training, higher motivation and better equipment; however, at 100 per cent capacity, the efficiency levels have averaged around 72 per cent,[4] as opposed to 85 per cent to 90 per cent in the United States. To the surprise of many, the most efficient factory within the CMB group is in Greece, where the level has reached 95 per cent. CMB management suggests that this startling level is because of the exceptional ability of the business unit manager.

While the results at the turn of the decade were gloomy when compared to predictions, it must be noted that, after only one full year in operation, the CMB group was already up to or nearing the results obtained for Carnaud S.A. after six years of turnaround. With investments in machinery, staff and market share among the highest in the industry,[5] the group has opted for a clear-cut strategy of aggressive growth, both internally and externally.

GAMBLING ON THE FUTURE

When CMB Packaging sold its steel operations despite their profitability, it made a conscious decision to limit itself to the production and sale of metal and plastics packaging and closures. Furthermore, CMB's chairman not only expressed the wish to see

----

4. An efficiency level of 72 per cent implies that, of every 100 units produced, only 72 are actually usable.
5. Investments in 1990 were equivalent to 7.2 per cent of total turnover, or 2.3 billion French francs.

CMB grow, but also to see it become a worldwide leader. While for many being a world leader signifies having the largest chunk of the market, to Descarpentries, the market share is simply a means to an end. For him, being the industry leader means:

- having the lowest unit production costs;
- having the highest return on investment;
- being the most innovative;
- having the best service (personalisation, delivery, quality); and
- having the lowest cost of money.

In order to achieve this, CMB has gone about acquiring market share at a rapid rate. To serve as an example, one can cite CMB's flexible packaging operations. Realising that this was and will continue to be an important type of product, CMB invested in and acquired a market share equivalent to 950 million French francs in just under two years, hence catching up with the market leader whose sales totalled one billion French francs. Internal investment is essential, but speed of action requires strategic alliances, even if CMB has a minority holding at the outset.

Yet the issue is not only one of being the biggest, but also being present with the right products for the right customers. With the creation of impersonal hypermarkets revolutionising the traditional chains of distribution, the individual middleman is being forced out of the market, leaving packaging as the primary intermediary between the consumer and the product. As a result, the packaging must not only protect the contents and the user, it must also inform and sell through attractive design and labels.

Based on this and the trends towards personalisation, CMB is choosing to stay out of the low-cost packaging market and focusing on made-to-order, high-quality products. In plastics, this implies concentrating on high performance plastics, plastics closures and flexible plastics, the combination of which is expected to grow at an average rate of 6–7 per cent per year.

In the beverage can segment, the situation allows less room for manoeuvre, the market being more or less dictated by conglomerates such as Coca Cola and Pepsi-Cola, who are seeking not only quality, but low prices. In the United States, the emphasis has been on aluminium cans, a trend gaining hold in Europe as well.

Adding to the complexity of the overall market situation is the ever-growing consumer awareness of environmental issues.[6] Not wishing to lose market share due to unclean or non-disposable products, CMB has begun awarding 'Oscars' to the most innovative products within the group. In 1990 alone, out of twenty-three projects submitted, sixteen obtained awards and six or seven pilot projects are now in the realisation phase.

In delegating responsibilities downwards, CMB has given itself the opportunity to become more flexible and thus more responsive to the needs of the market. In doing so it has also allowed itself to grow via acquisitions, as such a decentralised approach allows for maximum independence for any new unit brought in. Yet there is a danger of excessive internal fragmentation.

CMB is, in ideal terms, a European company. In reality, however, 'European' translates into Anglo-French, with the corresponding difficulties and rivalries this implies. The British are accused by the French of stubbornly remaining British in their outlook towards Europe and the world, while the French are, in turn, accused of being inflexible and chauvinistic. As already mentioned, steps have been taken to change such points of view, such as the creation of a Brussels headquarters and as much cross-Channel communication as possible, but acceptance of such steps takes time and they will undoubtedly be most effective with new recruits. As the company takes in more and more business units in the race to gain European and world leadership, the consolidation of one corporate culture will become increasingly difficult.

The creation of CMB Packaging is already being rated as a failure or success by both the press and its competitors. In fact, such a verdict will only be justified towards the second half of the 1990s, when the results of the steps taken will be measurable.

---

6.   Seventy-five per cent of all cardboard products are now biodegradable and hence suitable for recycling.

3 FAI SpA: The Challenges of Growth

Chapter 2 aimed to show not only the strategy opted for by a major multinational to confront the decade ahead, but also to bring to light the various types of problems or conflicts that can surface in a cross-cultural merger. At the root of these problems lie the challenges inherent in the creation of a new corporate identity that must, by definition, encompass the ways of the old companies as well as the differences resulting from the respective cultural heritages. Yet not all companies in Europe are multinationals: most, in fact, are not.

The challenges being faced by medium-sized corporations, often family run, are perhaps more acute, as they are increasingly finding themselves squeezed between the 'made to order' approach of flexible small operations on the one hand and the aggressive, low-cost multinationals on the other. Often lacking significant internal resources, the managers are faced simultaneously with creating a defendable competitive advantage and developing a corporate identity, an element often forgotten in the transition from a group of entrepreneurs to a significant competitive force.

Still remaining within the realm of industry, FAI SpA, situated near the city of Verona in northern Italy, provides an example of such a company. Still predominantly family run, FAI is finding itself catapulted into the big league, in combat with the world's leading multinationals on a global level. With strong products behind them, the management is now going through the difficult process of securing a profitable position within the marketplace and of making up for lost time with respect to the company's internal structure and identity.

DEFINING A BUSINESS

FAI, operating from two pieces of land totalling 130 000 square metres (of which 58 000 are covered), is involved in the assembly and sale of earth moving machines and parts. From factories in Italy alone, the company sells throughout the world (see Tables 3.1 and 3.2) and specialises in compact excavators suitable for construction and works in areas allowing for only limited manoeuvrability. Unlike leading manufacturers such as the US-based Caterpillar, or Japanese Komatsu, FAI is not represented in the very large tractor segment.

Table 3.1　FAI SpA: foreign sales as percentage of total

	1987	1988	1989
Finished product sales			
Italy	70.43	61.59	55.98
Exports	20.18	30.23	36.08
Totals	90.61	91.82	92.06
Spare parts sales			
Italy	2.84	3.13	3.12
Exports	1.11	1.31	1.87
Totals	3.95	4.44	4.99
Used sales	5.44	3.74	2.95

Table 3.2　FAI SpA's export market evolution

	Markets
1974	Yugoslavia
1975	South Africa, France, Denmark, Belgium, Holland
1976	Germany, Tunisia, Switzerland, Venezuela
1977	Austria, Turkey
1979	Ireland, Greece
1980	Portugal
1981	Algeria, Iceland, Nigeria
1982	Martinique, Morocco, Spain
1983	Saudi Arabia, Cameroon, Somalia, Oman, Taiwan
1984	Norway, Yemen
1986	Iran
1988	Canary Islands, Japan, Israel, Luxemburg

FAI's complete product range consists of the following:

'Rigid' loaders   These machines are equipped for digging holes up to 5 metres deep as well as for loading, and are suitable for day and night usage. FAI has an approximate 30 per cent share of the Italian market, but is beginning to encounter strong competition from UK-based JCB, a multinational with aggressive marketing tactics combined with low production costs due to economies of scale. FAI benefits in this segment from its reputation as an innovator (for example, it was the first to introduce a 4-wheel drive version). In addition, Ford and Case Poclain compete in this segment, but they both lack the necessary distribution and servicing network.

Articulated loaders   Considered to be one of FAI's 'leading edge' products, this loader is characterised by a high degree of versatility because of its digging and loading capabilities in tight spaces. In Italy, FAI is undeniably the segment leader, benefiting from a lack of competition as well as a technically strong product.

'Crawling' excavators   Operating on rollers as opposed to wheels, these excavators are equipped with a long arm capable of digging various materials up to 9 metres deep and within a 360° radius. Of all the segments in which FAI operates, this is the most difficult to penetrate, as every major manufacturer of earth-moving machines is present. FAI's position is further complicated by the fact that its crawling excavator has been known to have problems in the past and that its product line is not complete when compared to companies such as Caterpillar, Fiat–Hitachi or Case Poclain. Together, Fiat–Hitachi and Caterpillar control 50 per cent of the Italian market, a situation resulting in great part from their respective reputations for quality and servicing. Komatsu, the Japanese overall world leader, has a reputation for high quality, but it lacks the necessary distribution coverage.

Compact excavators   A recent innovation, the compact is equipped with the most advanced technology, including 4-wheel drive, and is particularly useful in carrying out construction, maintenance, snow ploughing and repair works in tight spaces. FAI and Bobcat are the Italian market leaders, but the segment is relatively undeveloped at the present time.

Mini-excavators   Originally developed in the United States, these are miniature versions of the crawling excavators used for jobs varying from gardening to the installation of gas and water networks to daily maintenance on construction sites and in factories. The mini-excavator has only recently arrived in Italy (1980) and as yet has a limited market. FAI benefits from a solid quality image, but, because of the market potential in this segment, all the major competitors are keeping a sharp eye on its evolution. The Japanese have significant experience in this segment and are estimated to have already produced 60 000 units, thus giving them valuable economies of scale as well as production experience. Eager to capitalise on this, FAI has already created a licensing agreement with Japan's leading manufacturer, Komatsu.

In addition to the five principal product lines described above, FAI also has a stake in three other companies. The first of these is CMI Srl, of which FAI owns 99 per cent. CMI occupies itself with the sale in Italy of used machines bought by FAI SpA. The second, FAI Firenze Srl, is responsible for the sale of FAI products in certain regions of Tuscany. FAI has a 99.8 per cent stake in this company. And finally, FAI Marketing Srl. With 24 per cent of the shares held by FAI, this company is concerned with the study, analysis and valuation of potential markets in Italy and abroad.

THE ROAD TO SUCCESS

The company's origins date back to 1914, when the founder began the distribution of Ford tractors in the area surrounding Verona and Padova. However, the first major step forward occurred in 1957, when Giovanni Bettanin, the founder's son, began the distribution of domestic and imported earth moving machines in Northern Italy. Not long after, and timed to coincide with the beginning of its own production of loaders, FAI SpA was officially created. Anxious to expand, FAI began innovating by being the first to make and sell 4-wheel-drive loaders. These were exported to nearby markets as early as 1965.

But FAI's real innovation was to come in 1979, with the creation of the FAI compact excavator. Though produced originally under the guise of a separate subsidiary, this company was fully integrated into FAI SpA in 1987–8.

Today, FAI has sales totalling approximately 190 million Italian lire and has some 750 employees. The bulk of this growth has occurred since 1986 (see Tables 3.3 and 3.4). As initially indicated, FAI's rapid growth both within Italy and in international markets has brought opportunities that are challenging the old ways of functioning and thinking. Because of the adaptability of FAI's products to the particular needs of Italy's construction companies and public services, which often need to carry out jobs in the narrow streets of historic centres, as well as the national coverage that the company has been able to gain over the years, Giovanni Bettanin

Table 3.3   FAI SpA: total sales 1968–90 (in millions of Italian lire)

	FAI SpA	*FAI Compact**	*Total*
1968	1 279	–	1 279
1969	2 046	–	2 046
1970	2 310	–	2 310
1971	1 944	–	1 944
1972	2 441	–	2 441
1973	3 551	–	3 551
1974	4 995	–	4 995
1975	4 585	–	4 585
1976	8 744	–	8 744
1977	11 820	–	11 820
1978	12 228	−21	12 207
1979	20 849	3 702	24 551
1980	24 371	5 841	30 212
1981	30 020	7 454	37 474
1982	36 247	8 325	44 572
1983	33 933	10 156	44 089
1984	36 126	11 943	48 069
1985	44 907	17 014	61 921
1986	52 604	28 236	80 840
1987	80 079	19 392	99 471
1988	–	–	141 814
1989	–	–	163 483
1990	–	–	190 000**

Notes:
* Consolidated with FAI SpA in 1987–8.
** This is a rounded estimate.

Table 3.4   FAI SpA: employees, 1980–9

	Senior managers	Staff employees	Factory	Total
1980	8	70	225	303
1981	10	74	221	305
1982	10	75	231	316
1983	11	69	227	307
1984	9	74	240	323
1985	12	91	312	415
1986	11	91	349	451
1987	12	106	398	516
1988	12	124	475	611
1989	16	162	553	731
1990	18	163	556	737

and his staff have been able to function in keeping with the entrepreneurial and family spirit that has reigned since FAI's founding. However, with the rapid growth in exports that has been witnessed in the last decade, FAI is coming into contact with the likes of British-based JCB, American-based Caterpillar and French-based Case Poclain. Competing with multinationals that have access to extensive internal financial and technological resources combined with well-defined strategies and corporate cultures requires, or rather forces, managers to sit down and identify what products they are selling, why they are selling them and what can be done to safeguard the position gained thus far. To do so necessitates a change in perspective that is often difficult to accommodate.

REVIEWING THE COMPANY

Production

At the heart of a traditional industrial company lies production and in this FAI is no exception. At present, FAI operates out of two production facilities, Noventa Vicentina and Este, the latter being also the company headquarters. The Noventa Vicentina factory contains the used parts warehouse and provides repair services. In addition, the larger parts of the final products (for example, the bodies of the larger loaders and excavators) are also made here. The Este facility, where over 60 per cent of the factory employees are to be found, contains the principal production line, including painting, electrical wiring, storage and shipment and the final assembly of all machines. Because the products assembled by FAI have numerous components that would require expertise and production capacity not held by FAI,[1] 65 per cent of the final product are brought in from outside.

The machines made require a significant lead time – on the order of six to eight months – thus forcing FAI to make-for-stock, as clients are usually unwilling to wait more than a few weeks for final delivery. However, thus far, almost all of the products are sold by the time they come off the production line. Yet, it is clear that such a system could backfire in the event of unforeseen circumstances or the arrival of a new competitor. Complicating the matter is the fact that FAI is not thoroughly computerised, hence necessitating the manual control of warehouses as well as manual production planning.

Sales and Marketing

It is not unusual to see industrial companies place little if any importance on marketing. Marketing has, in fact, been traditionally reserved for those operating in services and consumer goods. Yet, as was indicated in the case of CMB Packaging, the international economic and competitive factors being witnessed today are forcing industrialists to change their stance and look actively at what the consumer wants and then work backwards from that point. In the case of FAI, it is possible to see an example of what is occurring in many family run companies throughout Europe: the sales and geographic presence of the company have outpaced the existing structure.

---

1. FAI buys the motors, hydraulic systems and transmissions for its final products from third parties; these are then assembled into the bodies of the machines which are made in-house.

A quick overview of the present structure reveals a strong technical/ production orientation combined with a sales as opposed to a marketing staff. The key departments of the company are:

● after-sales service (technical);
● finance and control;
● internal organisation/information;
● administration;
● sales and marketing; and
● foreign affairs.

Looking at sales in greater depth, these are subdivided into 'Italy' and 'International'. Italy is in turn divided into three geographic areas, each one led by an area manager. Adjacent to the area managers in each of the three subdivisions are managers whose chief objective is to act as a market 'thermometer': that is, watching sales evolutions on a regular basis and monitoring clients. Finally, below the area managers are the agents and dealers (approximately fifty-seven within Italy). These sit down every year with FAI management to set sales objectives. However, few if any incentives are provided for the agents and dealers to actually reach or surpass these objectives. While the system has worked, the aggressive marketing strategy of a new entrant such as JCB could destabilise the entire network.

On the international side, there is a central foreign office that deals with contracts on a country-by-country basis. The objectives for each are set by the company president and marketing director. In those countries where FAI is strongest,[2] FAI has dealers which are monitored by FAI inspectors.

Thus, while FAI succeeds in covering 90 per cent of its own Italian territory as well as numerous countries throughout the world with a product that is well regarded in the industry, it is clear that, unless internal changes accompany the outward success, FAI will have difficulty in maintaining a competitive position based only on its product. Competing with multinationals is apt to require a

---

2. FAI's strongest foreign markets are France, Spain, Germany, Portugal and the UK.

clearly-defined plan of action and, equally important, a management understanding of how to win over a client. FAI has relied almost entirely on personal sales, scorning advertising and promotion. Both, however, will need to be incorporated into a new management philosophy.

Aware of these challenges, FAI has, in fact, made moves to bring in new blood, hiring one or two ambitious MBAs. Yet, while these new recruits may have the ideas and the knowledge to adapt to new competitive situations as they arise, their biggest challenge at the outset will be to win over employees and senior managers who have worked in the company for years – in some cases for decades. With respect to detailing a plan of action, greater strides have been taken to secure a defendable competitive position.

PLANNING FOR THE FUTURE

As is the case with many smaller and medium-sized companies, managers are turning to strategic alliances to safeguard their respective positions. Such is the case with FAI, which has struck up a partnership with Japan's Komatsu. Komatsu is world leader in the production and sale of construction and earth-moving machinery and has over 600 sales points within Japan alone. Eager to strengthen its position within Europe as well as to complete its product line[3] by adding FAI's product lines to its own catalogue, Komatsu has joined up with FAI in an agreement that allows each manufacturer to sell through the other's network. In addition, FAI obtains technological know-how by having a licence to make and sell Komatsu's super-compact excavator.

On an another front, FAI has been evaluating the possibility of going public so as to obtain a rapid injection of cash required for investments in plant modernisation and restructuring. In an effort to prepare for such a move, it has allowed one American merchant bank and two Italian banks to buy into the company (see Table 3.5).

---

3. Komatsu is particularly strong in heavier machinery.

Table 3.5   FAI SpA: ownership structure

	% shares
Valimsa Corp., S.A.	40
Giovanni Bettanin	15
Antonio Bettanin	10
Gigliola Tesei	5
SoPaf SpA	13.5
Arca Merchant Bank	11.4
Arca SpA	2.1
Kidder Peabody Italia Srl	3

Table 3.6   FAI SpA: income statement (in millions of Italian lire)

	1989	1988	1989/1988 % change
Net sales	163 483	14 1814	15
Cost of goods sold	134 308	113 902	18
Gross profit	29 175	27 912	5
Administrative expenses	8 736	6 091	43
Sales expenses	12 378	10 212	21
Operating income	8 061	11 609	– 31
Financial charges	4 319	3 778	14
Financial income	4 584	4 373	5
Other	1 045	– 82	– 1 374
Profit before taxes	9 371	12 122	– 23
Net profit	4 289	6 098	– 30

THE FUTURE?

Despite a slight decline in quality from the time when the company was small, FAI is nevertheless widely recognised as having a reliable product with a good level of quality control. In addition, it has established itself as an innovator, due in part to its strong research and development department. Judging from recent research carried out among existing and potential clients, these factors should certainly help procure a profitable future as they are regarded as being most important in the final choice of an earth-moving machine.

However, as with every company that exists, there are problems that need to be overcome. Perhaps chief among them is FAI's need to establish a strong corporate personality, preferably marketing-orientated, so as to increase worker motivation and lessen the relatively high employee turnover witnessed so far. Communication needs to be strengthened, both internally and externally: internally so that all have a common vision, and externally so that FAI take a more aggressive stand in the marketplace against the growing wave of international competitors.

4 The European Truck Manufacturing Industry:[1] An Industry Overview

The preceding two chapters have given some insight into the ways that corporate managers in Europe are evaluating the challenges and strategic options that face them as they prepare their companies to chart new paths into the twenty-first century. However, before going on to look at some other specific company situations, from different countries and sectors within Europe, it is interesting to pull back and take a more 'macro' perspective of an entire industry and to examine the changes taking place within it as the individual actors each aim to ensure their own profitable survival.

The introductory chapter has already indicated that the decade ahead will prove to be a testing ground for companies throughout Europe as they attempt to come to terms with rising costs, deregulation, increasing international competition and the erosion of traditional market structures as they know them today and have known them during the preceding decades.

In this chapter, I will give an overview of the European truck manufacturing industry, as it serves to illustrate how the creation of the Single European Market (SEM) has affected and will continue to dramatically alter the structure and the key success factors of an entire sector.

---

1. This chapter has drawn heavily on information provided in an industry note entitled 'The European Truck Industry in 1990: Preparing for the post-1992 era', by Frank de Haan and Hubert Thomassen (both MBA students, IESE, 1990), under the joint supervision of Prof. Leo Sleuwaegen (Erasmus University, Rotterdam and Katholieke Universiteit, Leuven) and Prof. Paul Verdin (INSEAD, France).

Defining the Truck Industry

Before embarking on an analysis of it, it is important that one has a clear understanding of what 'the truck manufacturing industry' actually refers to.

The truck industry is most often divided into four segments, each one being defined according to the Gross Vehicle Weight (GVW)–the maximum weight of the vehicle plus its load:

Car derived vans: GVW less than 3.5 tonnes;
Light trucks: 3.5–6 tonnes;
Medium trucks: 6–16 tonnes; and
Heavy trucks: in excess of 16 tonnes.

At the present time, the prices registered in each category range from 12 500 ECUs for a van to 30 000 ECUs for a light truck and 130 000 ECUs for a sophisticated heavy truck. In the present analysis, the focus will be primarily on trucks of 3.5 tonnes or more.

THE 1980s: A PERIOD OF RESTRUCTURING

The beginning of the 1980s witnessed a significant drop in total European truck production, due in large part to the collapse of the Middle-East and African export markets and a severe economic recession in Europe. The net result of this downturn was excess production capacity to the order of 50 per cent. However, beginning in 1984, a strong economic recovery began to reverse the trend, to the point that some manufacturers managed to attain full production capacity by the end of the decade.

In 1988, West European manufacturers produced 400 000 trucks and 1 250 000 vans, of which 88 000 and 150 00 respectively were destined for export. The remaining units were for the European markets which were, and remain, relatively free from non-European Community competitors, with the exception of the vans segment, in which the Japanese have successfully conquered almost 23 per cent of the total market.

Table 4.1   Production of trucks in Western Europe, 1980–93

	1980	1984	1987	1990	1993 *(est.)*
Data in 000s	500	336	356	345	360

Source: National statistics.

With respect to European competitors, the recession which opened the decade of the 1980s resulted in the beginnings of an industry shake-out and a re-evaluation of how to compete in the years to come. The highly complex industry structure visible today comes as a result of this process.

TODAY . . .

As it stands today, the European truck market is characterised by a high degree of cyclicality due to the fact that vans and trucks are capital goods whose replacement is easily postponed in difficult times. The demand for trucks remains a derived demand for which substitutes (for example, rail transport) are easily available, as was witnessed in Europe prior to 1987. Subsequent to 1987, new demand as opposed to replacement demand accompanied a growing economy.

The Users

Vans and light trucks are used primarily for local and regional delivery purposes, while medium and heavy trucks are used for long-distance transportation and heavy jobs, such as construction. With respect to shipping, companies use their own fleets, though jobs can be subcontracted, this really being a function of the size and degree of sophistication of in-house shipping departments as well as of the primary activity of the company (for example, a major industrial group can maintain a well-managed fleet of a hundred or more trucks). On the other hand, dedicated transportation firms range from owners of single trucks to companies with in excess of 200 trucks and/or vans.

While general transportation firms exist, increasing competition among hauliers has resulted in specialisation by type of goods, such as art works or inflammable chemicals. However, increased competition among hauliers has not only caused some to focus on market niches, but also to place increasing strategic importance on more efficient logistics (and hence lower costs) as well as increased international activity, to safeguard their position in an expanded geographical market.

An emphasis on cost-efficient logistics has resulted in a closer relationship between hauliers and dealers, as the former put pressure on the latter for better and faster repair service and maintenance, these items accounting for up to 25 per cent of a haulier's total cost, the rest being 50 per cent for labour and 25 per cent for fuel.

The Manufacturers

In order to understand the impact on the truck manufacturers of the trends in the various client markets, it is helpful to first understand how these usually structure themselves. Most of Europe's truck manufacturers divide their operations along the following lines:

- research and development (R & D);
- manufacturing;
- marketing, sales and distribution; and
- truck leasing and financing.

Table 4.2 Employment in the European truck industry: leading manufacturers, 1984–89

Company	1984	1985	1986	1987	1988	1989
DB	70 371	77 352	81 182	82 039	82 000	81 000
Iveco	36 263	34 585	36 053	35 962	38 110	37 800
RVI	40 000	40 000	36 000	34 792	34 151	34 000
Volvo	15 700	16 150	16 500	17 600	17 700	17 850
Scania	19 758	20 129	21 334	22 755	23 000	23 250
Daf	8 710	8 678	9 304	16 631	16 491	17 250
MAN	16 353	16 438	17 144	17 142	18 487	17 500

Research and Development

Technologically sophisticated trucks are more and more the standard in Europe as hauliers search for increased competitiveness and reduced costs. As a result, development costs for manufacturers have increased significantly, at present varying between 4 per cent and 8 per cent of sales, depending on the size and degree of vertical integration of the producer. Today, the development of a new product typically takes between four and seven years. However, once complete, the new product can be expected to have a life of ten to fifteen years and to require only limited investment for small improvements.

Recently, in the attempt by manufacturers to decrease their respective costs, the focus has been on possible economies of scale in research and development, particularly in light of the increased demands from clients in the areas of fuel efficiency, ergonomics and electronics. It is becoming more and more evident that the large competitors have a distinct advantage in this area when compared to the smaller players, thus forcing the latter to, on the one hand, focus on particular components, and, on the other, to form strategic alliances aimed at sharing R & D expenses. It is widely accepted that the production of the motor and the gearbox provide the most savings potential, with estimates for an efficient production line ranging from 50 000 to 100 000 units. The production savings possible on the other components remain difficult to ascertain.

Manufacturing

The main components of a truck are: axles, chassis, motor, gearbox and cabin. While in the United States most manufacturers are assemblers, subcontracting the actual manufacturing of parts, in Europe one finds a full range, from fully integrated manufacturers such as Volvo and Scania, who create up to 60 per cent of their sales value in-house, to assemblers such as Fiat/Iveco, for whom the percentage drops to as low as 30 per cent.

Industry observers tend to disagree on the exact efficient scale for production of the various components and final assembly. However, it is widely accepted that the production of the motor and the gearbox provide the largest potential economies of scale (estimates vary from 50 000 to 100 000 units per year for an efficient plant). On the other hand, the production of the cabin, axles and chassis, as well as the final assembly, are the least sensitive to production economies.

Table 4.3   Minimal yearly volumes for optimal production

Cabins	200 000
Frames	40 000
Axles	40 000
Engines	200 000
Final assembly	100 000

Source: Interviews.

Table 4.4   Estimated costs of manufacturing trucks, in percentages

Cab	14
Engine	20
Gearbox	10
Axles	7
Chassis	4
Line assembled components	35
Final assembly	10
Total	100

Source: Muller and Owen, 1981.

Table 4.5   Productivity indicators in the European truck industry, 1984–89 (number of trucks manufactured/total number of employees)

Company	1984	1985	1986	1987	1988	1989
DB	2.9	2.8	2.8	2.9	2.9	2.9
Iveco	2.3	2.9	2.6	3.0	3.3	3.7
Volvo	2.6	2.6	2.7	2.6	2.6	2.7
Scania	1.1	1.1	1.2	1.2	1.2	1.2
Daf	1.5	1.5	1.6	2.5	3.2	3.1
MAN	1.1	1.1	1.1	1.2	1.2	1.4

Source: National statistics.

It is to a large extent the aforementioned possibility of economies of scale that determine the outcome of the make/buy decision, though the contribution of each component to product differentiation also plays a large, and possibly increasing, role in such decisions, as each manufacturer seeks to adapt his products to the needs of the clients.

Marketing, Sales and Distribution

The marketing staff of the main European truck manufacturers usually find themselves involved in two activities: the creation of brand and product awareness, and the setting-up of a dealer network capable of handling final sales, distribution and after-sales servicing.

Thus far, with respect to the creation of brand and product awareness, the majority of the expenses have been concentrated in trade fairs and specialised journals, though, on some occasions, some companies have gone so far as to use television for the launching of new products. But, once again, the advantage goes to those with a large market presence who can rely on their widespread image as well as, in some cases, their fame in related business (such as is the case with Volvo, Daimler-Benz/Mercedes-Benz, and so on). This again is forcing the smaller manufacturers to seek strategic alliances that will facilitate the marketing and distribution of their products. The majority of truck manufacturers use a two-layer distribution system, selling to dealers via the use of a national importer.

Without exception, European truck manufacturers consider their dealer and service networks as one of the determining factors in their overall sales sucess, as can be witnessed by the fact that, despite a decline in the total number of manufacturers, a corresponding decline in the number of dealers (who usually remain committed to one brand) has so far not occurred.

Truck Leasing and Financing

As has occurred in many industries involved in the production of capital goods (for example, aircraft production, industrial machines, etc.), the rising costs to clients as well as the increasingly competitive environment has caused truck manufacturers to become engaged increasingly in the financing of their products, thus creating another mechanism designed to attract clients and bind them into a long-term relationship.

The functioning of such financing agreements varies in accordance with the size of the manufacturer. Some of the larger ones have already gone so far as to create their own financial services divisions which borrow money on the capital markets, while others often just act as middlemen, providing information and referrals between dealers, banks and final customers.

As the markets become more sophisticated, demanding and competitive, Europe's manufacturers will find themselves increasingly operating in areas previously unthought of, such as client financing, and so they will be in search of new capabilities that will ensure their survival.

... LOOKING BEYOND

The decade ahead will witness the most significant symbolic change with the creation of the Single European Market in 1992. This is for many a magical deadline when, overnight, the structure of the entire European economy will change as a result of the abolition of national borders. However, for most manufacturers in the truck industry, the impact of 1992 has already begun to take effect and has, as previously mentioned, already resulted in an overall streamlining of the industry which is expected to continue into the 1990s.

In fact, the general tendency witnessed already in the 1980s for manufacturers to rationalise manufacturing and obtain scale efficiencies by centralising production in fewer, more specialised locations has resulted in an increased average distance between factories and the final clients. Consequently, international distribution systems are rapidly evolving in which local centres are supplied from various production sites scattered throughout Europe. During the 1990s, this concept will demand more and more attention, exerting pressure on internal logistics systems, particularly as demand increases.

By the year 2000, industry analysts expect a 30–50 per cent increase in intra-EC trade, due to two factors:

1. The relaxation and gradual abolition by 1993 of quotas which limit the number of trips a haulier from one country can make into other EC countries within a given year; and
2. A dramatic reduction in the formalities, and hence delays, required at border posts by the introduction of the Single Administrative Document (SAD), which replaced the country-specific documents in 1988.

In addition to the above, the European Commission aims to allow for unrestricted cabotage (the freedom for a haulier registered in one EC country to collect and deliver loads between two points inside another EC country).

Yet these changes, aimed at facilitating cross-border business within Europe, are also accompanied by an increased environmentalist concern to reduce fuel consumption, toxic gas emissions and noise levels, as well as overall traffic levels. Switzerland and Austria have already enacted legislation to this effect, in the form of fuel and road taxes and decreased tax-deduction possibilities. The European Community is expected to follow suit in the near future.

This rapidly-changing environment has, on the one hand, stimulated the demand for international transportation and, subsequently, the demand for medium-to-heavy trucks, while, on the other hand it has increased the demand for better and more far-reaching innovations in truck design and truck specifications, to provide better freight capacity and reduced logistics costs. Truck manufacturers have thus found themselves with ever-more demanding and powerful clients and increased investments in research and development accompanied by shorter product life-cycles, thus limiting the period over which they can amortise these investments.

The Users

Present analysis indicates that the aforementioned focus on improved logistics and reduced costs, as well as internationalisation, is expected to continue for the next five to ten years. Full-truckload operations are expected to become increasingly competitive with significant market entry, while less-than-truckload operations are expected to become more concentrated in the hands of fewer pan-European networks, thus putting yet more pressure on the manufacturers for an improved and more sophisticated product. The pan-European companies have also shown signs of integrating forward into distribution.

Distribution

The issues that arose during the second half of the 1980s are apt to reinforce themselves and intensify, as users continue to seek improved service and maintenance. The truck manufacturers all agree that a solid dealer network serves as a strong barrier to entry, particularly for Japanese manufacturers who have so far been unsuccessful in entering the medium and heavy truck markets. The Japanese have, however, been successful in the car-derived van segment, taking advantage of their existing distribution networks (Toyota) and their ties with European car manufacturers (Honda with Rover).

The competitors

Other forms of merchandise transport exist primarily in the form of rail or combined truck/rail. The former, as can be seen from the figures provided in Table 4.6, indicate a general decrease in the use of railways during the 1980s, a trend which is expected to continue. However, the concept of truck and rail is presently being studied as a means to decrease road congestion and pollution. This may prove to be particularly useful for Alpine countries such as Switzerland and Austria and for Britain, once the Channel Tunnel is completed in 1993. Nevertheless, the combination of truck and rail requires a sizeable investment in national infrastructures and so it is a relatively safe assumption to make that reliance on truck transport will continue to increase into the 1990s.

At present, the majority of European truck manufacturers are characterised by strong market share positions in their home countries, aided by tariff and non-tariff barriers (such as technical specifications) and, in some instances, government subsidies (for example, Renault received 20 billion French francs from the French Government to compensate for accumulated losses, though it has since been obliged to return it). Those producers with relatively

Table 4.6 National rail and road transport in five EC markets (in billions of tons/km)

	1979	1982	1987	1993 (estimate)
France				
Road	94.6	77.1	89.9	102.9
Rail	70.0	53.9	51.3	50.4
Total	94.6	131	141.2	153.3
W. Germany				
Road	123.9	119.8	142.7	164.7
Rail	66.3	57.4	59.1	60.0
Total	190.2	177.2	201.8	164.7
Italy				
Road	81.6	94.9	108.9	125.6
Rail	18.4	17.7	19.3	21.5
Total	100	112.6	128.2	147.1
Spain				
Road	92.2	91.5	95.7	114
Rail	10.3	10.5	11.5	12.2
Total	102.5	102	107.2	126.2
UK				
Road	104.6	96.8	107	118.5
Rail	19.9	113.3	122.6	133.8
Total	124.5	210.1	229.6	252.3
EC Total	681.8	732.9	808	843.6

Sources: National statistics forecasts: BIPE, IFO, PROMETEIA.

Table 4.7 Selected market share data by manufacturer and by country, > 3.5 tonnes, 1987

	W. Germany	France	Italy	Holland
Daimler-Benz	48	20	12	23
Renault	2	40	0	2
Iveco	16	15	68	5
Volvo	4	10	4	16
Daf–Leyland	2	6	2	27
Scania	4	5	8	9
MAN	20	3	2	10
Others	4	1	4	8

Source: Dealer and manufacturer interviews.

Table 4.8   Estimated manufacturers' percentage exports
outside Europe, 1989 estimates

	% export of total sales
Scania	39
Volvo	35
Volkswagen	19
Daimler-Benz	17
PSA	17
Daf–Leyland	15
Ford	12
MAN	10
Renault	9
Iveco	4

Source: National statistics forecasts.

small home markets have, however, already been forced to establish themselves on a European level, in the hope of being better prepared for the possible consequences of 1992. Perhaps the manufacturers traditionally less prepared for the SEM are the British, who thus far have not concentrated on creating a strong European presence.

Most European manufacturers belong to large industrial corporations, some of which are diversified into a large range of industries, though the bulk are in the automotive area. The players, of which there are now only seven significant ones, vary in the scope of their respective product lines and the degree of vertical integration, as well as the extent to which they have each ventured into strategic alliances.

Daimler-Benz

The truck division of German-based Daimler-Benz (DB) forms one of Germany's largest conglomerates, with interests in areas ranging from cars (Mercedes) to aircraft (Dornier) and electronics (AEG). DB is at present European and world leader, marketing a full line of products, though it is particularly strong in the medium truck segment. The production is divided between Germany for medium

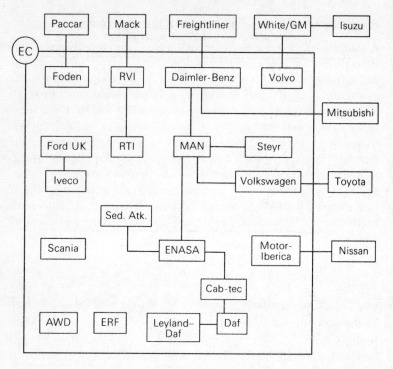

Figure 4.1   Linkages between European truck manufacturers

and heavy trucks, and Spain for vans and light trucks. In 1989, **DB** acquired **DTV**, an independent supplier of diesel engines, thereby increasing its degree of vertical integration.

Fiat/Iveco

Characterised by a low degree of vertical integration, Iveco (Fiat's truck division) remains a leading force in the Italian truck industry. In an attempt to strengthen its European position, Iveco entered into a joint venture with Ford UK in 1986, after having acquired the German Magirius Deutz in 1982. Though primarily an assembler, Iveco has extensive co-operation agreements with suppliers such as Eaton and Rockwell.

Renault

A leader in the French automotive industry, the state-owned Régie Renault has been plagued by problems ranging from labour unrest and subsequent strikes to a significant drop in government subsidies as a result of EC legislation. Renault declared accumulated losses of 5.32 billion French francs for the period 1984–86. In 1987, these losses were turned into profits of approximately 195 million French francs. A full-line producer, Renault has a strong presence in the American market, where it has a 45 per cent participation in Mack, as well as in Africa. In Europe, Renault remains a leader in the van and light truck segment, with an estimated 20 per cent market share, just ahead of PSA's (Peugeot/Citroen) 16 per cent. European production is centred in France, though with plants in the UK and Spain.

Volvo

Volvo, based in Sweden, is active in the automotive market as well as the medium and heavy truck market. Highly integrated, Volvo benefits from EC legislation because of its plants in Belgium and Scotland. In 1990, Volvo and Renault exchanged shares, with the intention of merging in the medium term.

MAN/Steyr

In 1989, MAN acquired the Austrian-based truck manufacturer Steyr, followed by the acquisition of the Spanish Enasa (maker of Pegaso trucks), thus making it a significant European player in the medium and heavy truck segments and complementing its access to vans and light trucks by way of a previous co-operation agreement with Volkswagen. However, the acquisition of Enasa (which was finally bought by Italian Iveco in 1990) had subsequently to be undone due to a ruling from the German anti-trust office, which limited MAN's presence in Southern Europe. MAN is nevertheless now in a position to offer a full line of products through its existing dealerships.

MAN has a relatively low level of vertical integration and has many of the same suppliers as DB, thus causing some speculation with respect to the degree of co-operation between the two leading German manufacturers.

DAF

In 1987, the Dutch-based DAF (the only European all-truck manufacturer) acquired the state-owned British Leyland, thus gaining improved access to the British market as well as to a broader product line, originally limited to the medium and heavy segments.

Scania

Scania is considered to share the same characteristics as its counterpart Volvo, though Scania's market is confined to Western Europe. An important asset of Scania is that it manufactures all its own components, hence controlling a sizeable spare-parts market and contributing to profits, which are used to subsidise the presently unprofitable car manufacturing segment.

The Americans

Subsequent to the crisis experienced in Europe during the earlier part of the 1980s, the American producers, who were present through UK subsidiaries, withdrew from the European market and now account for negligible imports, American and European truck standards being totally different.

The Japanese

The Japanese have succesfully entered the van segment, thus competing with Renault, but have been excluded from the truck markets because of their lack of dealerships as well as having different technical specifications.

Eastern Europe

Eastern European manufactures such as the Czech Tatra or the Soviet Zil have been unable to obtain a significant presence in Western Europe. As they lack adequate technology, it would appear that they instead represent possible acquisition targets for Western manufacturers.

An overview of the European truck industry provides a useful glimpse of the range of challenges that individual companies, in all sectors, can expect to face in this last decade of the twentieth century. For many, future success will not be a function of price, but of quality and service. Competition is increasing and will continue to do so for companies throughout Europe as they attempt to find their specific niche or as they act to gain the necessary volume that will allow them to survive, based, on the production side, on competitive costs, and on the consumer side, on the supply of a superior product adapted to the needs of the clients. The remainder of this book will look at specific companies from across Europe in an attempt to identify how each one is coping with its respective situations.

Part II
European Services

5 Zust Ambrosetti, SpA: Adopting a European Perspective

Between now and 1993, access to the international transport of goods by road will be totally liberalised and free of any quantitative barriers . . . The crossing of borders will be done without requiring extended stops. These circumstances will have the net effect of increasing the efficiency of road transporters as well as making them more competitive than rail transport. On the other hand, it is important to underline the problems that transporters will have to face: infrastructure saturation and the difficulties arising from environmental control.
(Dr Eugenio Belloni to the International Conference on road and rail transport, Venice, 15–17 June 1990)

Chapter 4 brought to light the key macroeconomic trends that will be affecting the truck manufacturing industry during the decade of the 1990s. But the future of the truck manufacturing industry is inevitably tied to the potential of its client sectors. One of the largest segments served by truck manufacturers is that of merchandise transporters, whose function it is to ensure the safe and efficient transport of goods on behalf of individual and corporate clients, within Europe and throughout the rest of the world.

Characterised by extreme fragmentation, with many companies only operating one or two trucks, transporters are becoming increasingly concerned about the impact of two trends: the rapid saturation of Europe's infrastructure, in particular the road systems, and the growing environmental protection movements. The former limits the capacity for growth while the latter imposes restrictions on much-needed road construction, thus forcing the market leaders to seek new, efficient and clean alternatives to their existing services. Add to this the impending liberalisation of the transport sector (1993), under the supervision of the European Community, and it is quite easy to understand that the market leaders of the transport

73

industry have little time left to secure a strong competitive position. Not only is competition expected to increase in foreign sales, but also within each country from foreign competitors seeking new markets. As the competition increases (intra-Community traffic went from 55 per cent of total transport sales in 1982 to 62 per cent in 1988), the number of takeovers and mergers are also expected to increase as part of an effort to rationalise the overall industry structure and thus obtain greater potential economies of scale in production, logistics, organisation and marketing.

AN OVERVIEW OF THE MAJOR INDUSTRY TRENDS

With the passing of time, the transporters' clients are finding themselves focusing more and more on the production of high-value-added products in an effort to make up for the lack of technological differentiation prevalent in many industries. This being the case, these clients are actively seeking ways to decrease the transport time necessary between factory and consumer. This, in turn, is causing a phenomenon observable in many industries: the gradual squeezing out of intermediaries and the elimination of unnecessary loading and unloading during shipment. As companies gradually adopt the concept of integrating transport into the overall production chain, they will also realise the advantages of the Japanese 'just-in-time' delivery method. For those transporters unable or unwilling to meet these requirements, the future will be uncertain.

ZUST AMBROSETTI

Northern Italy provides a challenging backdrop for examining in greater detail the means by which transporters are gearing up for the 1990s as not only is it an area still in the midst of rapid growth, but it is also one whose borders with neighbouring countries are, for the most part, situated in the difficult transitways of the Alps. This makes the life of a transporter that much more arduous due to increased travel times and correspondingly higher costs.

Zust Ambrosetti (ZA), with headquarters in Turin and operational management in an industrial area of Milan, began its

Table 5.1 Zust Ambrosetti: Italy's top ten transporters, 1990 (in millions of Italian lire)

Company	Value-added	Sales	Pre-tax profits	Cash flow	Labour costs	Depreciation	Investment in trucks
Domenichelli	94 839	246 320	2 557	6 983	89 178	4 854	17 523
Saimavandero	84 705	445 569	7 133	9 211	81 946	5 211	9 187
Zust Ambrosetti	**82 740**	**438 947**	**26 908**	**17 879**	**52 255**	**4 781**	**10 211**
Tripcovich	66 396	341 429	11 760	11 634	52 379	3 726	6 539
Danzas	63 231	949 508	716	3 987	55 050	5 065	8 448
Bartolini	48 184	189 088	5 653	13 624	25 756	10 680	14 132
TNT	47 749	112 752	3 623	20 878	21 823	19 239	2 334
Merzario	38 552	371 245	(16 189)	(14 486)	49 031	1 777	17 846
Maritan Borgato	35 497	59 502	950	2 580	31 767	2 054	4 194
Arcese	33 974	166 183	1 223	7 705	24 257	6 972	23 424

Source: Tuttotrasporti.

Table 5.2　Zust Ambrosetti: the development of road and rail traffic in Europe, in percentages

	1975	*1988*
Road	58.4	73.7
Rail	15.1	9.9
Sea/canals	26.5	16.4
Total (bn tonnes)	631.2	1 026

Source:　1990 Conference on International Road–Rail Transport.

operations in 1906. Though ZA suffered extensive damages to its property during the Second World War, it has managed to recover to the point of being Italy's leading transporter, with sales of the order of 440 billion Italian lire (see Table 5.1) and over 28 000 clients. Yet such an extensive client base is not enough to make ZA's managers feel secure in their relative market position, for the simple reason that today's clients still choose their transporters primarily on the issue of price, thus creating a volatile and uncertain turnover for the transporters.[1] In fact, while ZA and its competitors believe that the cost of transport should be included in the initial estimates of a product's production costs, this is a practice still rare among the transporters' clients. As a result, and to gain a competitive edge, ZA has opted for a global approach to its business, not just in terms of the markets served, but also with respect to the services offered.

Today, with a total of twenty-one branches in Italy alone, ZA operates 500 trucks, or 3000 tonnes per day, on 250 different truck routes. In addition, ZA ships 150 000 tonnes of merchandise per year by sea as well as over 600 000 automobiles per year on its 6000

1.　Many clients calculate the price of their goods without taking into consideration the cost of transport. This being the case, these clients have no choice but to squeeze the transporters on their fees, to secure the highest possible margin for themselves. ZA managers and their colleagues believe that the cost of transport should, in fact, be included in the initial estimates of a product's production cost.

railway cars. As a member of IATA, the International Airline Transport Association, ZA is present in all the world's major airports. With services ranging from express delivery of packages to the transport of dangerous goods, works of art and animals as well as moving projects cargo, ZA is in a position to meet virtually any kind of request from its clients. Compared to most transporters, ZA offers a complete range of services. Yet because the client is price-sensitive, such a breadth of product line does not allow the ZA management to sit back and relax. Instead, ZA's directors believe that the next step is to begin to change the mentality of its clients by forcing them to think in terms of quality and reliability. This in turn will, in theory, invert the sales process by getting the clients to come to ZA, rather than the reverse, as occurs at the moment. But changing a mental attitude is a challenge that cannot be met without first having the internal structure and resources to match.

CLEANING HOUSE

Industry has long since been viewed as an area where the key to success is the command a manager has of his production line. Marketing has, in fact, been disregarded or, at best, packaged with sales. But today's competitive situation, with its proliferation of technological know-how and its product standardisation, has invalidated this approach to the extent that the adoption of a marketing dominated managerial style is now becoming the rule rather than the exception.

ZA is aware of the need to create its own innovative and sustainable marketing philosophy and it firmly believes that it is this that will ultimately determine its future success. As a first step in this direction, ZA has recently undergone a restructuring programme, the central idea of which is to organise on the basis of markets served. Today, ZA consists of four divisions: overseas air and sea (intercontinental); Europe; motor vehicle transport; and domestic (Italy). Each division is responsible for market forecasting, administrative procedures and the implementation of senior management strategy guidelines. Above the divisions, one finds the directors, whose function it is to develop corporate strategy, evaluate investment proposals, supervise logistics and develop new marketing strategies.

Contrary to the form of its old organisation, the new structure is highly centralised. The justification for this lies in the assumption that a centralised approach (which nevertheless will allow for sufficient subsidiary autonomy) is necessary to create a coherent corporate identity and strategy and to allow for potential economies of scale to be taken advantage of. The latter is most noticeable in the area of information systems.

Believing that information and its wise application is one of the future keys to success in the transport industry, ZA has invested in a system that at present comprises a mainframe biprocessor, 38 departmental mini computers, 320 video terminals, 180 PCs, 350 printers and 15 data transmission lines, the latter connected to the Italian public network, ITAPAC. In addition, each subsidiary has at its disposal an internal system for the control of daily operational procedures and is now plugged into a central mainframe so that a client can be kept informed, in real time, as to the whereabouts of its products. The information available is cross-referenced by client, postal code, type of merchandise transported, and destination. Furthermore, ZA has gone so far as to connect its system with those of its leading clients so that shipment orders can be placed and tracked without the bother of sending over a salesman.

Yet, as can be expected with the installation of such a vast network, problems do arise. The system is providing information on a continuous basis on all of ZA's clients; however, ZA's management is finding itself flooded with an indigestible amount of information, much of which should not be wasted. With the objective being to identify its clients' needs, both now and in the future, ZA has developed an internal control system that will direct the correct information to the appropriate managers, while maintaining necessary client and company confidentiality. This is essential if the marketing philosophy being adopted is to be functional rather than theoretical.

With an internal management system now suited to the aggressive and competitive market situation in which ZA finds itself, the next frontier is to improve client services. Aware that most of its competitors are small operators without the needed infrastructure or resources to offer more than just the shipment of a product from point A to point B, ZA is gambling its future on the creation of a global network.

Believing that a network of correspondants is not enough to control a geographic area, ZA is working on establishing partnerships with companies willing to invest in areas such as the creation of new loading terminals, data bases and research and development as well as on integrating its direct correspondents with its foreign representative offices. Through a controlled network, ZA and its partner can then profit from the exchange of information and technology as well as take advantage of economies of scale arising from the more efficient handling of merchandise. One such example is ZA's partnership with a leading French transporter (SCETA). Aside from providing additional capital, the French partner has allowed Zust Ambrosetti to gain access to twenty different arrival points within France. In this way, ZA is closer to the client and thus able to provide a cheaper and more efficient service.[2]

However, while efforts across the French border may be forthcoming, the situation in Austria, an important access route to Eastern and Northern Europe, has proved to be more complex. The Italian–Austrian border has been the site of numerous blockages due to the different laws regulating the transport industry in the respective countries. These regulations have contributed to significantly higher costs and security risks due to the need to change drivers and to the many hours necessary for border control. Complicating the issue is the fact that Austria, as well as Switzerland and Yugoslavia, the two other important border countries, are not in the European Community and are not expected to be in the immediate future. As a result, leading Italian companies such as ZA are seeking ways to resolve the incompatibilities and ensure the smooth flow of traffic in the years to come. As it turns out, Austria and Switzerland are also countries where the 'green' movements (environmental protectionists) are exceptionally strong, thus putting pressure on the respective governments to promote the increased of alternative merchandise transport systems before pollution and resulting problems get out of hand.

---

2. By having terminals closer to the client, ZA avoids unloading and reloading at intermediate terminals, thus decreasing transport costs as well as increasing security and speed.

LOOKING FOR AN ALTERNATIVE

The need to find environmentally clean means of transport for the shipment of goods, as well as to find ways to meet the expected growth in demand for such shipments (200 per cent expected by the year 2003; 300 per cent by 2015), transporters such as ZA have recently been placing a lot of emphasis on the possibility of combined road–rail shipment. Taking into consideration ZA as a multi-modal transport operator (MTO) with its extensive fleet of trucks and railroad cars as well as its wholly owned facilities, such an alternative could prove to be highly interesting in that it would allow for the most advantageous use of both road and rail, providing a solution to the dual problem of road saturation and pollution as well as increasing security for the transport of dangerous, fragile or valuable goods and decreasing the necessary investment in infrastructure.

The basic concept behind combined road–rail transport is that goods are shipped by rail on the long-haul stretches of the journey, while road transport is used for shipment from the train terminal to the various clients. This said, there exist two methods of implementing the rail transport: accompanied and unaccompanied. The former implies that the entire truck and its contents, plus driver(s), are loaded on to a train, while the latter implies that the shipped goods are transported in containers suitable for both rail cars and road transport. Accompanied transport provides a short term solution, as it resolves the problems arising from containers which do not fit all the existing rail cars. However, it is costly and therefore, once technical standards have been simplified and streamlined within Europe, unaccompanied transport is by far the better solution.

Combined road–rail transport has, in fact, existed since the 1950s, but thus far accounts for only 4 per cent of the total shipments within Europe. This percentage is somewhat higher between France and Italy (9 per cent) and Germany and Italy (19 per cent) due to the advantages of rail transport in crossing the Alps, yet it has never really been fully accepted by the transport industry as a whole.

At the root of the problem lies a seemingly intransigent difference in mentality between the transporters and the railways: on the one hand, the railways have apparently refused to invest in the necessary terminals for the loading and unloading and transferral of goods, as

---

CEMAT – The National (Italian) Association for Combined Road-Rail Transport

CEMAT was created by FS (Ferrovie dello stato), the Italian railway (65 per cent), and by a group of independent transporters (35 per cent), in 1953 with the aim of promoting combined road–rail transport through the management of what today number twenty-three intermodal transport terminals. In 1989, of the 120 000 shipments made, 59 462 were within Italy and 61 443 were international. Of the combined shipments undertaken, CEMAT at present has a market share estimated at 44 per cent.

---

well as in client service. Such investments have been further complicated by the fact that each country has its own legislation and technical standards governing its railways. Many of these technical specifications are often incompatible with those of neighbouring countries.[3] And no Community legislation is expected to come through in the foreseeable future to improve the situation, though pressure is mounting, as witnessed by the number of high-level transport industry/EC conferences which have taken place, aimed at addressing these particular issues.

Looking specifically at ZA, it and other leading transporters have encountered difficulties in promoting combined road–rail transport due to the traditional barriers of mistrust that have prevailed in past decades. However, as co-operation increases and pressure to find alternative means of transport mounts, these barriers are gradually breaking down. The burning issue is who has the control of the clients: shipping company or railway? From ZA's perspective, it

---

3. As an example, the British, French and Italian railways are not equipped to handle all types of railway car. Furthermore, the quality of the railway infrastructures differs greatly. As an indication, the average speed for the shipment of goods by rail is 80 kph in France and Germany, but only 37 kph in the rest of Europe.

should be the shipping company as that is in the best position to decide on the most efficient routing and means of transport.

Combined road–rail transport necessitates, above all, a significant investment in logistics and compatible informations systems (an estimated 3 billion ECUs will be necessary to streamline the European railways). To achieve this is going to require a European

---

Some Road–Rail Competitors

A look at two of Europe's leading road–rail transporters highlights their orientation towards the maritime markets as opposed to the road transport segment, as well as the problems they face in dealing with the railways.

Intercontainer

Intercontainer, a privately held company with sales totalling the equivalent of 523 billion Italian lire and a fleet of 3800 railway cars, is Europe's leading intermodal transport container company. With headquarters in Basle, Switzerland, it employs 280 people from seventeen countries, who are responsible for the transport of containers in ports and private terminals. One of its major aims is to improve the reliability and efficiency of the European railways. Presently, however, it is encountering difficulties due to national differences which are creating problems at border crossings.

Novatrans

French Novatrans is 66 per cent owned by SNCF, the French national railway, and derives its business 50/50 between domestic and international transportation. Its network and terminal system is structured so as to service the major French harbours. Its primary function is, however, to act as an intermediary between road transporters and SNCF and to negotiate tariffs with SNCF. This is becoming increasingly difficult as it finds that SNCF is faced with higher fixed costs and decreasing productivity.

(as opposed to the current nationalistic) mentality that will allow for the creation of European networks. It would seem that ZA's management is heading in this direction, but it will be a difficult task to pursue if their international competitors do not follow suit.

What is certain is that, with the globalisation of the world's markets, the transport industry will have to follow suit in order to keep abreast of its clients' needs. This is particularly true when taking into consideration the idea that most of the products of the year 2000 do not yet exist. With the standardisation of technology, the emphasis will be increasingly on high-value-added products that will be transported in smaller quantities. It is with this in mind that ZA has its own packaging subsidiary whose brief it is to develop new packaging methods according to client specifications.

With a strong infrastructure, extensive resources and its management philosophy in place, ZA's goal is to use what it has now to change both clients' and competitors' philosophies: the former in such a way that they include the cost of transport in their production estimates and the latter so as to facilitate the creation of cross-border networks.

6 Banco Comercial Português: Putting Marketing at the Forefront

The opening up of an entire economy can present opportunities often dreamed of by entrepreneurs who have an ideal and a mission; it is a chance to break free and attempt to alter the status quo, revolutionising the way people think and act. Yet such attempts often fall short of their objectives as ambition outpaces reality. In 1984, the founders of Portugal's Banco Comercial Português[1] recognised this risk, but nevertheless pushed on, aiming to be Portugal's leading private sector bank in record time. It was a race against the clock from the very beginning as they recognised that, in order to survive, they would not only have to convince their target market of BCP's superiority relative to other institutions, but also gain a sufficiently strong internal position to be able to defend themselves against the onslaught of European competition that would herald Portugal's entry into the European Community in 1986. Today, there are few people who would not concede BCP's success, a success due primarily to the accepted but often ignored principle that 'the customer knows best', applied through a careful market segmentation process and corresponding niche strategy. The managers of BCP are not wizards or magicians, but instead individuals who have the intelligence and the daring to apply traditional concepts in such a way that they will produce results. The strategy opted for is best summarised in the following words, taken from the 1989 annual report:

---

1. Throughout the text, the Banco Comercial Português will be referred to as BCP.

84

The confidence of our shareholders and the outstanding dedication of our staff has enabled us to build a strong financial services group in just four years. This rapid expansion has been founded upon a commitment to quality service and in developing relationships with all of our clients.

Today, having successfully established itself as a leader in its own retail market, BCP is looking towards rapid international expansion as well as internal diversification, two goals which confirm the management's aggressive and ambitious but well-thought-out strategy, and whose results are already in evidence: the group includes leasing and factoring companies, two major insurance companies, investment banking and assets management operations. The focus in this chapter will be on the banking activities.

In order to truly understand the challenges that BCP has been confronting from the start, it is necessary to understand the politico-economic environment in which BCP was born and, to a large extent, still functions.

Of all the European Community countries, Portugal is undoubtedly the least known or understood as well as one of the poorest and smallest. It is a complex society with a recent history that still weighs heavily on its conscience and from which only the younger generations are beginning to succeed in freeing themselves. This underlying complexity, which is filled with contradictions, only further proves the daring and the success of BCP's strategy.

Portugal and its leading business community members are making giant strides forward in an attempt to catch up with the rest of Europe. These giant strides are visible everywhere, from the building of new roads (such as the Oporto–Lisbon highway) and airports (Oporto) aimed at strengthening the country's weak infrastructure, to the promotion of foreign investment in services and industry in the hope of creating a few strong niches in which it will be possible to compete with the leading European Community countries and, in particular, Spain, a country which itself has undergone dramatic social changes and economic development since the death of General Franco and which has a predatory tendency to view Portugal as a natural extension of its market.

However, despite the recognition that rapid changes must be made if Portugal is not to become an economic dependency of

Spain, the internal social, economic and legal environments are not always forthcoming.

Turning more specifically to the Portuguese banking industry, the contradictions remaining from past political events are easily visible. While the Government of the Socialist President, Mario Soares, and the Social Democrat Prime Minister, Cavaco Silva, wants to see rapid changes, the existing legislation, in an attempt to please all parties, continues to act as a legal maze characterised principally by ambiguity. One of Soares' platforms has been and continues to be the privatisation of industries nationalised under the brief Communist regime that came to power in 1975. Such a policy implies a significant liberalisation of the economy. However, the legislation provided for lacks coherence and succinctness regarding the opening of the financial sector to private investors and entrepreneurs. As an example, the legal definition of the various institutions making up the financial sector does not coincide either with the operations actually allowed or with European Community definitions (for example, regional development companies can, in fact, act as monetary institutions accepting deposits; brokerage companies can act as credit entities, and so on). An effort is being made to rectify this situation, giving way to the idea of universal banking, that is, commercial banks and investment banks will not be differentiated. Furthermore, while foreign investment is regarded as almost a necessary evil, the government has stipulated that 75 per cent of the employees of all credit institutions must be Portuguese; this not only serves to discourage large-scale foreign investment, but is also in direct opposition to European Community laws. With respect to the requirement that 75 per cent of the staff be Portuguese, it is worthwhile noting that Portugal lacks a skilled workforce, particularly among those generations that grew up under the right-wing dictatorships of Antonio Salazar and Marcelo Caetano, the latter being overthrown in 1974. It is therefore not surprising to find that the average age of BCP's staff of 2000 is thirty, compared to competitor institutions where it is significantly higher.

Adding to the contradictions in the financial sector are the varying restrictive monetary measures put in place. Aimed at combating a relatively high rate of inflation (on the order of 10 per cent in 1991), the government had a policy of instituting tight credit restrictions and high compulsory reserve requirements; banks are still required to keep 17 per cent of their deposits on reserve with the central bank, Banco de Portugal, an institution whose role is expected to pass to a more supervisory function as opposed to the tight control experienced during the 1980s. Credit restrictions, the government's key monetary policy instrument, were abolished in 1990, but were replaced by a request that all banks decrease the lending growth rate. The situation in the financial sector, banks in particular, is further aggravated by the fact that the majority of the actors are state institutions. Run as such, the nationalised banks have never been motivated either by profit or customer satisfaction and have, instead, lobbied strongly against any initiatives by BCP, an institution largely viewed as a threat to their own security. Thus far, the nationalised banks[2] have proved to have a certain power, as is evidenced when BCP announced an interest-bearing cheque account. The leading banks did not hesitate to make their distaste known, succeeding eventually in convincing the government to limit such an interest rate to 4 per cent, an amount rendering BCP's new product essentially null and void. However, as proof of their daring and stubbornness, BCP countered this move by offering new products linked to treasury bills, a move which was facilitated by BCP's extremely high level of automation. It would seem that BCP was at least one step ahead of the competition, but for how long?

As long as the competition is limited to the state banks, BCP is in a very good position, for reasons that will be examined in depth later in this chapter. But one of the results of the attempt at liberalisation, initiated in 1983, when the then Prime Minister Mario Soares introduced legislation enabling the private ownership of banks and insurance companies, was the arrival of multinational banks from abroad. Quick to respond to the new laws,[3] Manufacturer's Hanover and Chase Manhattan of New York joined the existing foreign banks Lloyd's, Crédit Lyonnais and Banco do

---

2. Since 1975, the twenty-two state banks have, through various mergers and acquisitions, become eight. This process of consolidation is still continuing as the inevitable process of privatisation continues, bringing to light the inefficiencies of past operations.
3. In February 1984, applications were accepted for the creation of new banks, provided that investors could satisfy the 1.5 billion-Escudo minimum capital requirement.

Brasil, all three of which had operated in Portugal prior to 1974 and had managed to survive the turbulent years between 1974 and 1976. BCP was the third bank to be approved, followed by Barclay's Bank, Banque Nationale de Paris, Citibank, Générale de Banque and, from Portugal, the Banco de Comércio e Indústria (BCI). BCI, thus far, has been unable to compete effectively with BCP due to its lack of a clearly-defined market strategy.

Founded in Oporto, the industrial capital in the North, in June 1985, BCP began with a startling paid-up capital of 3.5 billion escudos, 2 billion more than the legal requirement established by the government. This capital was fairly evenly divided between a few hundred individual investors and private companies. Today, BCP has over 20 000 shareholders and is the largest on the Lisbon Stock Exchange, with 12 per cent of total capitalisation.

From the beginning, the BCP founders wanted to create a bank known for innovation. The issue was, how? Hindsight allows us the privilege of omniscience and, as a result, a certain power to criticise. As it turns out, the criticisms one can make today of BCP are few and relatively trivial in retrospect; those that can be made of the competition are, on the other hand, significant.

In Portugal, lending is tied to the deposits a bank has as opposed to the demand for credit. Realising this policy would be likely to remain in place, the President and Chief Executive Officer of BCP, Jorge Jardim Gonçalves, stipulated at the outset that, if he were to participate, BCP would have to promise to go into retail banking, thus guaranteeing access to retail deposits. The demand was met and he began on what many considered a risky venture.

The state banks, characterised by poorly located branch networks, a high level of problem loans,[4] low levels of capitalisation

---

4. Due to government pressure, the state banks had invested heavily in the old colonies (for example, Angola and Mozambique, both of which have been characterised by political instability and civil war) as well as in uncompetitive industries such as textiles and shoes. Today, up to 10 per cent of these banks' debts are deemed irrecoverable. In addition, the state banks are required to make high dividend payments to the government. Finally, the state banks are overstaffed and under automated; the average age is high and the level of motivation is low. However, any dismissals are blocked by the unions.

and high operating costs (3–4.6 per cent of average earning assets as opposed to the European Community average of 1.5–2 per cent) ridiculed BCP's entry into their domain and scoffed at the 1 billion escudo investment in advanced information systems.

But BCP pushed on, concentrating on developing a strong corporate culture, comparable to the 'white shirt–blue tie' syndrome of IBM, aimed at creating a financial group that would provide the customer with what he/she wanted. The problem was how to identify what the customer wanted when the majority of the potential customers had no idea of the options available. Hence, the first step was a detailed and accurate segmentation of the Portuguese market, a concept previously unknown in Portuguese banking circles, followed by consumer education.

Having succeeded in segmenting the national market, BCP is focusing increasing attention on the second, third and fourth phases of its initial strategy, phases that will ultimately determine whether it will become a European financial group or whether it will remain a successful regional bank. All the options eventually chosen must meet BCP's policy of low risk financial management.

The second phase consists of developing a banking network that will guarantee access to foreign exchange, a cornerstone of any bank's internationalisation process. Lacking the size needed to do so through the creation of foreign branches, BCP has opted for an off-shore banking system based on the island of Madeira. Such a strategy allows for a presence in the international markets without the inherent costs of branches; furthermore, not being subject to exchange controls or taxes, a degree of legal flexibility is assured.

The third phase remains less well defined, though an outline of its eventual form is gradually becoming visible. In essence, BCP views the third phase as allowing for the intervention of foreign capital, though in limited and controlled quantities. This remains a sensitive issue because, although BCP wants to see itself develop into a European presence, it still wants to remain a Portuguese group, a concept pivotal to its corporate philosophy and in line, to a certain extent, with the Portuguese view of the world beyond: perhaps the rest of the industrialised world is more sophisticated in its approach to markets and consumers, but we can do as well, if not better within our own borders. In this respect, BCP is aiming to satisfy clients, shareholders and employees, many of whom regard foreigners with a contradictory mixture of respect, awe and discomfort (the eternal presence/threat of Spain and its relative economic power cannot be overlooked in these sentiments).

In an effort to satisfy these mutually exclusive goals, BCP so far is opting for small foreign participations, pointing out that the key is not the size of the investment, but the nature of the joint venture; BCP views any international transaction limited to the exchange of capital as purely a defensive move against possible take-overs. In addition to any possible participations (the Banco Popular Español has 1.5 per cent of BCP's capital and the two banks operate jointly in France, where they are aiming for the large immigrant populations from both Spain and Portugal), BCP today boasts of 40–50 worldwide correspondent banks, all chosen for their reputation as financially solid and efficient banks, rather than for their price. In its dealings with international markets, BCP is expecting that the Portuguese government will maintain its promise of harmonising laws with those of the European Community[5] and will, furthermore, introduce a central depository and a continuous price system, therby reducing the operational gaps that presently exist between Portugal and other financial markets.

Provided the third phase proceeds in a controlled and manageable environment, BCP sees the fourth phase as consisting of a significant presence in the North American capital markets, for foreign entities not based in the United States. Eager to increase the pace of the group's development, BCP has already entered into agreements with such institutions as Morgan Stanley and Morgan Guaranty Trust of New York.[6]

This aggressiveness in moving ahead is based on a justified fear: the liberalisation of Portugal's financial markets will, as already mentioned, result in stepped up international competition. For an

---

5. Portugal became a full member of the European Community on January 1st, 1986. Such status implied the acceptance of the Single European Act of 1985 as well as of the Second Banking Directive, designed to pave the way for the elimination of all national protective legislation by January 1st, 1993. Whether or not the timing will still be maintained is, as yet, uncertain.

6. As an example, Morgan Stanley guarantees the liquidity of BCP's American Depository Receipts (ADRs), which are deposited in a foreign account held by Morgan Guaranty at BCP.

institution without the minimum critical level of assets and volume of transactions, it will be difficult, if not impossible, to keep pace with foreign institutions who already have a solid international reputation and presence and who have an infrastructure built up over decades. These banks already have a competitive edge in foreign exchange and investment management and can succeed without a major network in Portugal simply because of their respective reputations, which usually precede them.

As a result of this influx of foreign investment, it is predictable that Portuguese banks will lose internal market share and will be forced to reduce their profit margins as well as to specialise in specific areas, thus becoming regional banks. Further complicating the issue is the fact that, in accordance with European Community law, financial institutions will no longer have legal limitations to their capital participations in other financial entities. This is expected to lead the way to the creation of financial conglomerates. BCP is, in fact, gambling on this and has therefore ensured that its group is a major actor in all the key segments related to banking, such as leasing, insurance, asset management and merchant banking.

It is clear that BCP has the makings of a European institution, if not a global one, but there remains a burning question: how did they accomplish this in so short a time period and can they maintain the pace? To answer this, it is necessary to examine in detail the realisation of the initial concept of a retail bank catering to a well-defined and meticulously segmented market.

SEGMENTATION AT WORK: THE INDIVIDUAL CONSUMER MARKET

Having decided that penetration of the retail market was of vital importance to the future strategy of BCP, the founding managers were faced with the dilemma of how to attack the Portuguese consumer market in such a way as to gain the consumers' confidence and, simultaneously, educate them.

Portugal has approximately 10 million inhabitants, the majority of whom are concentrated on the seaboards, the areas most conducive to business and tourism, due to the temperate climate and the vicinity of the two major cities, Lisbon and Oporto. While Oporto is characterised as a relatively rich industrial city, Lisbon remains the centre for international business, particularly in services, the sector with the most promising future. The interior of the country, primarily agrarian, lacks any major centres as well as easy access, thus remaining somewhat removed from events in either Lisbon or Oporto.

Such a brief overview of the demographic profile is enough to suggest that the point of departure for an institution wishing to begin a new business and develop it quickly is indeed in the two major cities.

Using databases and government statistics, and with the aid of external consultants, the founding managers subdivided the consumer retail market into four major segments, based on income, as opposed to geographic location:

A – the top 1 per cent with an extremely high net worth;
B – high-net-worth individuals, estimated at 4–5 per cent of the total population;
C – individuals of medium income (estimated at 15–20 per cent of the total population; and
D – low-income households.

As one might reasonably suspect, the division along income lines coincides with the geographical spread of the population; the first three segments are concentrated in the cities and on the coast while the fourth segment remains dispersed throughout the country, difficult to identify and to reach.

The next stage was to decide on the initial target market. The top 1 per cent of the population consists of a group of people who have very specific needs with respect to portfolio management and who seek a highly personalised, sophisticated service. These are individuals who usually have more than one account, some of them often in either Swiss or Spanish banks. Catering to their immediate needs was deemed as too risky for BCP as the market potential was limited, and failure to satisfy customers could seriously prejudice the future of BCP's operations.

The low end seemed untenable on various counts. First, as mentioned, it was and continues to be difficult to reach. Second, and most important, this class is made up of individuals with a low level of education, often not beyond elementary school, and who have a general mistrust of institutions such as banks. Rather than put money in an account, they would just as soon spend it on a house or land. Furthermore, if they were to put their savings into an account, it was most likely to be with a government institution such as the Caixa Geral de Depositos, the national savings bank, which benefits from a network of over 450 branches. It was felt that BCP's ideal of wishing to offer a differentiated and innovative service would be likely to fall on deaf ears.

Having ruled out the top and bottom segments, it was then an issue of deciding where to strike first: the high-net-worth individuals or the medium-income individuals? As it happens, BCP now serves the top three segments; however, it was felt that the high-net-worth individuals would offer the most promise in the beginning. For a bank just starting out, this segment offered a potential market large enough for the existing staff to handle and to test new concepts. Furthermore, it was an easy segment to identify, and finally, preliminary market research had shown that this was the income group least satisfied with the services offered by competing banks. While the top 1 per cent had the amounts necessary to open accounts in Switzerland or elsewhere, these individuals found themselves stuck with what the market had to offer.

TARGETING THE HIGH-NET-WORTH INDIVIDUALS

In early 1991, the 'Particulares' division of BCP (the division catering to high-net-worth individuals) had approximately 40 000 households as clients, out of a potential 150 000, or 5 per cent of the 3 million Portuguese households, roughly equivalent to a market share of 25–30 per cent in terms of deposits. (BCP maintains that, in financial terms, their total market share rounds up to approximately 35 per cent.) All in all, these are staggering figures to have obtained in only five full years of operation. Wherein lies the secret?

While not wishing to belittle BCP's effort, the inertia of the competition cannot be overlooked. At the time of BCP's founding, the state banks lacked a strategy, be it towards the consumer or towards product innovation; they did not, in fact, offer any products, merely traditional cheque and savings accounts. They appeared as if in a vacuum, oblivious to the consumer or the changes in the surrounding economic and political environment. The national banks' service was and continues to be poor, relying on unmotivated and inefficient methods when compared to modern information systems. On the other hand, the three foreign banks, though able to take advantage of strong infrastructures, lacked a country-specific approach to Portugal; their strategies were and still are determined by headquarters thousands of kilometres away. Thus the conditions for attack could be said to have been optimal.

On the other hand, BCP's efforts contributed greatly. Recognising that there is often a certain inertia on the part of the consumer to change banks, as this can often create havoc with one's personal accounting, BCP aimed to make the process as easy as possible.

With a sales force of ten people (five in Lisbon and five in Oporto), BCP systematically attacked the target segment through the use of a four-step process:

1. An initial mailing, based on information provided in available databases, to inform the potential customer of BCP's existence and its products.
2. Telephone contact to arrange for a personal visit by a member of the sales force to the individual's house or place of work.[7]
3. A visit by a member of the sales force.
4. An invitation extended to the client to visit the agency.

Once persuaded into BCP's offices in either Oporto or Lisbon, the potential customer was struck by the luxury of the surroundings (up to 1000 square metres of marble and granite) and the efficiency of the 20 or so attendants. From there, it was a question of explaining why they should choose BCP and reassuring them in their decision.

Aware that one of the many problems with the competitor banks was an impersonal, often impolite service, with no degree of continuity, BCP from the outset has placed a great deal of emphasis on assigning an account manager to each individual.

---

7. The telemarketing staff is usually made up of university students who, once having gained experience, move up to the sales force and then to become account managers.

From the day this manager is assigned, he follows all the transactions of each client, thereby creating a feeling of trust and confidence. Thus far, no other bank in Portugal has matched this service. Furthermore, BCP feels it important that the client be esteemed and so, to contribute in this effort, the bank introduced the gold VISA card 'Prestige', another first for Portugal.

In light of the success of the 'Particulares' strategy, BCP offers now more and more products and services to its high-net-worth individuals, including investment planning, interest-bearing cheque accounts and telebanking,[8] as well as traditional cheque and credit services.

Today, it is clear that the leading banks underestimated BCP's initiative and, as a result, they are starting to take notice, particularly in light of their own possible privatisation in the years to come. Word of mouth in the upper market segments is still very effective in Portugal, where communities are tightly knit and seemingly 'omniscient'. BCP has, in fact, greatly benefited from this, allowing it to dispense with advertising initially and causing it to have to raise the required minimum average account balances for the 'Particulares' accounts. At the outset, the minimum was established at between 100 000 and 200 000 Escudos. Since 1985, the amount has gradually been moved up to 600 000 Escudos. Those individuals who do not meet this requirement are now transferred to another section of the bank, the 'NovaRede', whereas in the past, prior to NovaRede's existence, they were invited to close their accounts.

From the initial two agencies, BCP has expanded to thirty-two, with which it estimates that it covers up to 80 per cent of its target market. Hoping to arm itself against intensified competition, BCP would like to see this number increased to fifty. However, increasing the number of agencies is not enough to guarantee the future.

Today, BCP has a solid market share in the high net-worth-market – enough to enable it to expand upwards into the top 1 per cent market segment, which it serves through its 'Private Banking' network, these being agencies that require a minimum 10 000 000

---

8. Through telebanking, a client can conduct all major banking transactions via the telephone.

Escudo deposit.[9] Yet, a high market share does not guarantee customer loyalty. As the cost of getting additional clients increases each time, BCP's focus is moving towards finding ways of locking its existing clients into a long term relationship.

To do so, the 'Particulares' division is aiming to centralise all possible services in its agencies in such a way that a customer will have his insurance policies, mortgages, credit cards, portfolio management, and so on, all in the same file, at the same agency and with the same account manager. Once a client has reached this stage, it is doubtful he will have the will to move all or part elsewhere. This approach is already under way and proving successful, particularly as BCP is able to take advantage not only of the non-existence of such a service in other banks, but the generally poor image and mistrust of insurance companies who have yet to offer products adapted to the consumer. It is in the creation of such a network that the wisdom of the initially high investments in a centralised information system comes to light. Each employee, having at his side a microprocessing terminal as opposed to a 'dumb' terminal, can instantaneously access a client's file and provide up-to-the-minute information. The issue now is how successful competing banks can or will be in copying BCP.

However, BCP has higher aspirations than just becoming a niche bank, catering to the top 5 per cent of the Portuguese population. In order to grow and gain the critical mass volume necessary to become a European presence, BCP began to look not only at locking in its existing client base, but also at expanding downwards to the medium-income segment and smaller family companies. This, however, brought to light certain problems of a legal as well as a marketing nature.

From the legal perspective, BCP was not allowed to create a new institution bearing the word 'bank' within its name. This is, in and of itself, a surmountable problem. But deserving more attention was

---

9. The Private Banking division, aside from catering to a very select group of individuals, offers essentially the same services as the 'Particulares', though with a heavier emphasis on portfolio management and with separate client receiving areas, arranged like the living room of a private house. The Private Banking division is closely tied to the off-shore banking unit on the island of Madeira.

how to target a medium-income individual within the existing structure and not make the 'Particulares' clients feel as though their bank was losing prestige, one of the key initial selling points, while simultaneously preventing the new clients from feeling like second-class citizens.

NOVAREDE – EXPANDING THE TARGET MARKET

The marketing implications of a new division were by no means a small matter and had to be dealt with quickly and effectively if BCP's expansion strategy were to continue along the predetermined lines. While wanting to maintain the elitist image already firmly adopted, a compatible yet different position had to be found, without creating an altogether new bank. To help resolve the problem, extensive market studies were conducted to discover what it was the new client was seeking in a bank.

The results of the tests indicated that the medium-income individual was concerned primarily with three elements: quality and speed of service; control over his/her account; and the vicinity of agencies to either residence or place of work. Taking this into consideration, BCP managers held a few brainstorming sessions and came up with the idea of creating an extensive network of smaller agencies which would offer exactly this, while still maintaining the high-quality service BCP was known for. It was decided that this network of agencies would require a strong image, reflecting innovation and speed, but still tied to BCP, at least at the outset. The name finally chosen for this network was 'NovaRede – Banco Comercial Português'[10] (literally translated as 'new network'). The logo is designed in such a way as to distinguish itself completely from the original BCP agencies, yet still maintain BCP's name visible. As the success of NovaRede increases and the division gains a solid image and reputation of its own, it is regarded as a perfectly feasible alternative to eventually drop the Banco Comercial Português from NovaRede's logo. Whether or not this eventually occurs, however, NovaRede will remain an integral part of

------

10. On the logo, 'Banco Comercial Português' is written in subscript.

BCP, with the same standards and the same concept of a group-wide integrated infrastructure.

NovaRede is a young division of BCP, which is perhaps what makes its task seem that much more complex for, in many ways, it is upon the NovaRede that BCP is placing its hope of obtaining the necessary deposit volume spoken of earlier. Thus, while there is an obvious need to offer new and innovative products to the consumer, product development is not necessarily the area requiring the most investment. After all, adapting the products of 'Particulares' to NovaRede is a fairly simple procedure. Instead, the necessary areas of investment lie elsewhere for the time being: personnel training and number of agencies. Without the former, quality service cannot be maintained, without the latter, NovaRede will not be fulfilling one of the primary needs of the target consumer: proximity.

As mentioned, BCP has given great care to creating a strict corporate culture. NovaRede, as part of BCP, has not escaped such treatment, though the culture created within NovaRede can be said to be slightly different. The overall corporate philosophy stems from the President himself, whose wish it is to breed a corporate culture based on quality in which the smallest of details are as important, if not more so, than the overall scheme of things. Within the NovaRede, new recruits spend six weeks on a course learning sales techniques. During this course, they are not only given a full presentation of the BCP group, but are also given tips on such things as how to dress and how to address a client. Following this course, the recruits are then placed for two weeks in an agency located anywhere in the country. Only after this are they able to take up their final position. However, to prevent laziness or excessive job comfort from setting in, employees can be called at a moment's notice to change position as well as geographic location, creating a type of continuous 'revolving door' within the various divisions. When it comes to evaluation, it is done on a regular basis by the immediate superior. BCP has no central personnel department, having decided to delegate employee career management to the respective division heads.

With respect to the proliferation of NovaRede agencies, BCP appears to be proceeding at breakneck speed. With approximately a hundred agencies after only a year's operation, NovaRede hopes to have nearer 300 by the end of 1992, many of which it hopes to set up in residential suburbs, an area long overlooked by the competition, who have traditionally situated themselves in business centres. Where does this optimism stem from?

Studies indicate that 35 per cent of Portugal's cheque account holders change banks during the course of a year. Of this 35 per cent, 60 per cent change to NovaRede. Relying on these statistics as well as on the power of advertising and word of mouth, NovaRede's management is confident that their expansion plans, though ambitious, are feasible. It is, however, worth mentioning that the opening up of bank agencies became more complex in late 1990.

In part seeking to take advantage of the apparent success of the new commercial banks and in part to control their expansion, the government approved new legislation whereby any bank wishing to open a new agency would have to pay an 'entry' fee of 40 000 000 Escudos per agency in Oporto and Lisbon and 20 000 000 in other areas. These sums can, in fact, prove to be prohibitive for those entities without a solid client base. As it turns out, BCP does not regard this legislation as an obstacle. Quite the contrary, it could prove to be beneficial to them, at the expense of the weaker state banks.

NovaRede, in its first year of operation, succeeded in obtaining 100 000 accounts. Based on their success and the available statistics, as well as the actual structure of each agency, the government entry fee is deemed insignificant and easily recoverable. As opposed to competitor banks, whose agencies are usually large in terms of both surface area and staff, NovaRede's agencies average 100 square metres, with a staff of five. These five people are trained to handle all transactions, thus eliminating the need for specialists such as foreign exchange cashiers or administrative personnel. Furthermore, the 'back office' functions are all handled at the client counter through individual microprocessing terminals, equipped with access to the bank's central mainframe. The net result of such an agency structure is a much lower average cost of operation than that of the competition.

The proliferation of NovaRede agencies is expected to occur essentially in two distinct phases. The first consists of attracting potential clients through its reputation for quality and efficiency and, unlike the 'Particulares' division, advertising. In fact, in the latter half of 1989, NovaRede began an intensive campaign which has since been copied by various other institutions, though with much less encouraging results. This campaign consisted of, on the one hand, nationwide coverage in all the key media, and, on the other, a technique aimed at creating suspense: for the first month, neither BCP's nor NovaRede's name appeared anywhere. The reader was given bits and pieces of information or shown the future logo, all of which came together at the end of the month to explain what NovaRede was.

The second phase, already begun, is derived from the approach adopted by the 'Particulares' division and aims eventually to 'lock' the client into NovaRede's system by offering a global solution to banking, leasing, credit and insurance as well as the payment of bills. In fact, it is perhaps the automatic payment of monthly bills such as telephone, rent, or electricity that most ties in the customer, as changing any or all of these can be confusing and time-consuming.

BCP is quite obviously banking on the NovaRede to solidify its position in the medium-income market segment and to use this as a base for further expansion into such areas as insurance and leasing, where it hopes to take advantage of its prestige as well as its extensive agency network, assets the leading insurance and leasing companies cannot claim as yet. As time goes by and Portugal's population becomes wealthier and more international, BCP predicts it will be increasingly difficult to distinguish between the medium- and high-net-worth individuals – a phenomenon which, from their point of view, is already occurring. As a result, the products offered by the 'Particulares' and the NovaRede will coincide more and more, though the marketing distinction will be maintained. Ultimately, who goes to which division will be a function of how much they want to maintain as an average balance, as opposed to their monthly salary.

In parallel to the consumer banking division, BCP has placed a comparative though more cautious amount of effort into developing the complex corporate banking market, a segment which, in Portugal, is still characterised by instability and psychological barriers to innovation.

ATTACKING THE CORPORATE MARKET

Almost the whole of the Portuguese economy (98.5 per cent) is made up of small and medium-sized companies, most of which are concentrated in the textiles and shoe manufacturing industries, located in the centre and north of the country.[11] Of the remaining 1.5 per cent, 500 companies can be considered multinationals, primarily of foreign origin. Many of these, such as Procter & Gamble, the American consumer-goods manufacturer, have only recently begun to invest in the Portuguese market. The multinational market presents, in certain respects, less of a challenge than the small and medium-sized companies, despite multinational companies' need for sophisticated financial management.

BCP's Corporate Banking Division, which caters specifically to multinationals and larger corporations, consists of one office in Lisbon and one in Oporto, both with a very small staff. Unlike consumer banking, the success of serving multinationals is based almost entirely on the bank's ability to provide a tailor-made product which meets the client's specific needs. As a result, each potential client is evaluated on a case-by-case basis, the initial criteria being size and ownership, followed by the profile of the financial director. Obtaining a client whose financial manager has little responsibility, as is often the case when they are obliged to report to a headquarters in another country, requires time and effort which BCP does not regard as being sufficiently profitable.

BCP's corporate banking has adopted a slow growth approach in line with its controlled risk policy. However, the Corporate Banking Division also recognises the possibility of remaining a peripheral bank with respect to the international markets – a possibility that has increased since 1992 is with us. At that point, all national regulations, which so far have inhibited the development of the financial sector in Portugal, will disappear, giving way to supranational legislation from the European Community. The essence of the new European legislation is the concept of 'home country rule': any financial institution meeting the legal requirements of its home country, provided the home country is a member of the European Community, will be able to conduct business throughout the Community without further government approval.

Multinationals have a habit of spreading their financial portfolios among various institutions throughout the world, from commercial

---

11. Small to medium-sized companies are those that have less than 500 employees and annual sales of less than 5 billion escudos.

banks to investment houses. While BCP has enjoyed a certain lead time relative to the competition, it will be hard pressed to gain the necessary international capabilities required by multinational clients. The problem arises yet again of how to remain a Portuguese bank for Portugal, yet gain sufficient international status and prestige to be treated as an equal with the leading European financial institutions. While this issue appears more-or-less resolved on the consumer banking side, it has yet to be tackled fully on the corporate banking side.

Turning to the small and medium-sized companies market, the situation is radically different. Why? Until 1974, Portugal's economy was all but closed to the outside world. Under the governments of Salazar and Caetano, an effort was made to limit all contact with foreigners, particularly in the area of business. Rather than look towards Spain and the rest of Europe, attention and resources were focused on the African colonies, Angola and Mozambique, both areas beset by revolution through the 1960s and 1970s, until their independence in 1975. The result of such a policy was to create a wave of scepticism towards anything European or American and to inhibit seriously the technological progress of key industries such as farming and textiles. With the fall of the Caetano regime in 1974, Portugal entered a new phase of political and social instability. The independence of the colonies caused over a million Portuguese expatriates to return to their homeland within a matter of months. Most of those returning had left everything they owned behind, and so found themselves having to start afresh back home. In a country of ten million inhabitants, an overnight 10 per cent increase in the population posed tremendous strain on what was then a very weak system. From 1974 until the early 1980s, Portugal continued to have an inward focus, socially, politically and economically, to deal specifically with the problems posed during the mid-1970s. It was only in 1983, when the then Prime Minister Mario Soares announced plans to restructure the economy, that Portugal began to look at what was happening within its neighbours' borders. But, by then, it was already too late for an entire generation. An unwillingness to accept change and innovation had firmly established itself among a large majority of the country's population, including senior managers. While Spain was rapidly gaining on France and Italy by promoting foreign investment, Portuguese managers continued to run things as they had prior to 1975, an era in which everything, from prices to market shares, were tightly controlled. The concept of marketing was not adhered to, nor were basic principles of production and quality control, or analytical accounting and pricing. The rapid opening-up of Portugal, heralded by its becoming a full member of the European Community, did nothing to help the situation at first. These same managers saw foreign companies gradually come in and completely alter the structure of their respective markets, as they had known them for decades. This resulted in a sense of apprehension and even aggressiveness towards outsiders, as opposed to the sentiment that something could be learned as well as taught.

Today, younger managers, as they move up to positions of control in family-run companies, are attempting to rectify the situation through the creation of foreign alliances, executive training and so on. But, as the state banks have discovered, many of the small and medium-sized companies are no longer salvageable. With factories out of date, no marketing to speak of and balance sheets destined for bankruptcy, they will either die an accelerated natural death or be bought out by stronger competitors who have the cash and the will to restructure their competition.

Facing a situation of this kind, it is hardly surprising that BCP has no desire to be the number one company in this market segment. Rather than aim for market share, BCP has adopted a strategy coherent with its overall policy: offer quality and personalised service to those who meet the bank's standards with respect to financial management and competitive situation.

FUTURE PROSPECTS?

The Banco Comercial Português finds itself today in a position of strength. Since its creation in 1985, BCP has succeeded in creating a strong balance sheet, due primarily to its conquest of the deposit market, as opposed to being lending-driven and despite relatively high start-up costs. It has, in fact, gained a 5 per cent market share of total deposits and a 4 per cent market share of total loans.

After conquering the high end of the consumer market through its offer of a personalised service, efficiency and quality products aimed at a global solution to all the consumers' needs, BCP went on to tackle the medium-income segment, an endeavour which has proved to be equally successful and which continues as NovaRede strives to gain access to deposits throughout the country.

However, the fact remains that BCP is, by most standards, a small bank operating in an unsophisticated financial market. As an added complication, the Portuguese market is viewed as an extension of Spain, a country where the financial institutions have had more time and experience to develop solid infrastructures.

BCP wants to remain, at all costs, a Portuguese institution and hence avoid the large influx of foreign capital, that is beginning to happen to those state banks which are being privatised. Yet it wants to be a force on the European and even global capital markets. Not wishing to take on the risk and cost of establishing agencies in countries around the world, BCP will have to find ways of attaining its contradictory objectives and simultaneously fight off the new competition that is being created by the unification of Europe.

The options available, as seen from BCP, are quite varied:

- Reach more of the Portuguese immigrant populations through further development of its off-shore banking unit in Madeira. Though already begun, this will require considerable investment in both staff and products as well as international marketing efforts.
- The creation of joint ventures in narrowly-defined areas with foreign institutions meeting the quality criteria of BCP. This could provide a way of getting access to foreign expertise and foreign markets without jeopardising the identity of BCP itself. One such joint venture being examined is with the CARIPLO (Cassa di Risparmio delle Provincie Lombarde) of Milan in the area of mortgage credit. CARIPLO, despite being state-owned, is characterised by a broadly similar ambition to BCP, but has the advantage of benefiting from a European wide financial empire.
- Strengthen its position in major foreign capital markets, including getting itself quoted on key stock exchanges.

Whether BCP should choose one or all of the above to cope with a difficult future, it is certain that its application of traditional marketing theory in an innovative and aggressive format, together with its taking a gamble (and subsequent reliance) on high technology information systems, has put it at the head of Portugal's financial sector to lead the way into a new era.

Table 6.1   Banco Comercial Português (BCP): key figures

Year end	Total assets (in bn escudos)	Net profit (in bn escudos)	EPS (escudos)	Dividend (escudos)	Yield (%)
1987	129.7	1.7	77.3	60	1.7
1988	296	4.66	172.5	200	5.6
1989	519.22	10.24	227.6	110	3.1
1990	801.25	13.74	233.7	110	3.1
1991 (F)	–	19	287.9	130	3.6

Note:
F = forecast.

Table 6.2   Banco Comercial Português (BCP): profitability ratios for Portugal's six largest banks (all figures in percentages – 1988)

	CGD	BPA	BES	BPSM	BTA	BCP
Interest income/AEA	16.05	13.97	14.8	13.3	14.34	11.12
Interest cost/AEA	10.27	10.39	10.42	10.46	10.26	6.46
NII margin	5.78	3.58	4.38	2.85	4.08	4.66
Fee income/AEA	0.26	1.72	1.02	1.3	1.14	2.56
Operating costs/AEA	(1.73)	(3.33)	(3.03)	(4.57)	(3.32)	(3.96)
Provisions/AEA	(2.90)	(1.23)	(0.36)	(1.71)	(1.06)	(0.23)
Net profit (in bn Escudos)	26.3	2.8	3.5	1.3	1.0	6.7
Return on assets	1.28	0.24	0.39	0.17	0.16	3.85
Return on equity	22.81	15.56	16.39	8.5	6.69	17.23
Equity/total assets	6.45	1.63	3.07	2.0	3.07	13.15

Notes:
CGD = Caixa Geral de Depósitos
BPA = Banco Português do Atlántico
BES = Banco Espirito Santo e Comercial de Lisboa
BPSM = Banco Pinto e Sotto Mayor
BTA = Banco Totta e Acores
BCP = Banco Comercial Português
AEA = Average earning assets
NII = Net interest income
Source: Swiss Bank Report Equities Group.

7 Amsterdam Airport Schiphol: Creating a World Mainport

As the plane took off to the south and then turned back on itself, I could see the small terminal building, recently finished, flanked on one side by the tarmac and single runway and, on the other, by a car park the size of the terminal itself. Leading away from the airport was a two-lane road running east–west. Gradually, the plane gained altitude and before long, we were well above the clouds, oblivious to all that was happening 30 000 feet below. Then, looking out of the window as we penetrated further into French airspace, it was suddenly possible to see the criss-cross pattern of numerous jet trails (I could count up to six at a time) and, at one point, I could even identify a Swissair Airbus heading south, most likely on its way from London to Geneva or Zurich. We were just off the Normandy coast, with a view of France on one side and England on the other, heading into the most congested airspace in Europe: the quadrangle that is formed by Amsterdam, Frankfurt, Paris and London. It is virtually impossible to fly across Europe without crossing into the airspace of one of the countries included in this geographic area (France, Luxemburg, the United Kingdom, The Netherlands, Belgium and Germany).

Landing in Amsterdam, we took a somewhat circular approach which had the advantage of letting me examine Schiphol Airport from the air. It was clear that we were arriving at an airport which was not to be ignored. Surrounded by four runways, at least two eight-lane highways, a train line that serves as the main artery between Paris and Amsterdam, numerous hangars and cargo facilities as well as farms and the ever-present canals, a huge terminal building sprawled out like a giant hand. At touchdown, I was struck by the number of Boeing 747s in view, whose national flags extended from Indonesia to Brazil to the United States.

Being used to airports such as London's Heathrow, I was expecting to find chaos once inside the terminal building. Instead,

I found an extremely neat, well-signposted and uncongested arrival hall in which it took me exactly five minutes to clear Customs and be out. Once free of Customs, my next objective was to find the way to my hotel. As it turned out, I could choose from the bus, the train, a taxi, a minibus or, of course, the usual rental cars to be found the world over. Having decided upon the train, I followed the necessary signs and realised I was had reached the platform without having had to go out into that day's sub-zero temperatures even once. A very successful journey!

SCHIPHOL AIRPORT: WHAT IS IT?

Legally speaking, Schiphol Airport is a joint stock company whose capital is held 76 per cent by the state, 22 per cent by the city of Amsterdam and 2 per cent by the city of Rotterdam. The airport is run, however, as a limited liability company and is thus required to show a yearly profit; Schiphol does not receive any subsidies for its investment projects. Technically speaking, however, Schiphol is much more. Conceived of as a major airport destined to serve its surrounding geographic area, it is presently planning to become a world 'mainport': a global transport hub serving Northern Europe, for people and cargo from around the world, where it will be possible to connect to planes, trains and ships. In the words of the Board members:

> Masterplan Schiphol 2003 policy proposals published in 1989 specify and underpin the planned expansions of Schiphol's facilities up to the year 2003, based on Schiphol Airport's main port strategy. This strategy aims to boost further Schiphol's important role as a driving force in the Dutch economy, subject to limits set in the interests of prudent environmental and conservation policies. The key objective of the main port strategy is that Schiphol should maintain its present position as one of the leading airports in Western Europe, against the background of increasing competition within Europe. In view of the relatively small size of the Dutch domestic market, the further development of Schiphol as a hub for intercontinental and European traffic should be stimulated. (Schiphol Airport Authority, *Annual Report 1989*)

With over 200 000 transport movements per year, Schiphol Airport is presently ranked as the number five airport in Europe in terms of passengers and number four in terms of cargo handled (see Table 7.1). With respect to area and population, it is equivalent to a small town of approximately 50 000 inhabitants: 36 000 people are employed by companies operating on the airport premises[1] and 1800 are directly employed by the Airport Authority.

Table 7.1   Schiphol Airport: European ranking
of the top ten airports, 1990

Passengers (millions/year)	
London*	64.8
Paris*	46.8
Frankfurt	29.4
Rome*	18.4
Amsterdam	16.5
Madrid	16.4
Stockholm	14.9
Zurich	12.7
Copenhagen	12.1
Dusseldorf	11.9
Cargo (000s tonnes/year)	
Frankfurt	1 106
London*	951
Paris*	872
Amsterdam	605
Zurich	256
Brussels	n.a.
Rome*	243
Madrid	221
Cologne	163
Milan*	144

Note:
* Includes several airports.

___

1. This figure includes flying staff of KLM Royal Dutch Airlines, KLM Cityhopper, Martinair, Transavia and Air Holland, but not the flying staff of any other airlines. Also not included are the 6700 employees of Fokker Aircraft, whose offices and hangars are located on the east side of the airport.

In the past, KLM, the Dutch national carrier, and the Schiphol Airport Authority have been lucky in that their objectives have coincided. KLM have pursued and continue to pursue a strategy of total world coverage. Their network, together with the other eighty or so scheduled airlines operating in and out of Amsterdam, allows Schiphol to boast of service to over 200 different destinations spread across ninety countries.

WHAT THE AIRPORT INCLUDES

The Schiphol management has just undergone an important phase of restructuring as it gears up to prepare for the twenty-first century. Led by a Board of Directors, the new structure comprises four business units: Landside, Terminal, Airside, and Facility Management. Designed to increase decision-making speed and efficiency, the new business unit structure aims to delegate more responsibility to lower management levels and thus enable senior management to concentrate on policy decisions. Ultimately, it is hoped that this increased efficiency and quality will result in improved profitability and a 15–20 per cent increase in productivity.

SCHIPHOL AIRPORT'S INCOME

The Schiphol Airport Authority obtains the bulk of its income from airport fees, which are in turn made up of aircraft landing fees, passenger fees and parking fees[2] (see Table 7.2). However, in

---

2. The amount charged for landing and take-off is a function of the aircraft's weight and the number of passengers on board the aircraft at take-off, the maximum being for aircraft of over 20 000 kg. In such a case, the fee is 254 florins plus 17.10 fl. per 1000 kg or part thereof for weight in excess of 20 000 kg. The passenger fee is set at 16.95 fl. per *departing* passenger and 1.50 fl. for transit passengers. With respect to parking charges, there is no fee for a period of under six hours. Any period exceeding this time limit is charged at the rate of 2.65 fl. per 1000 kg per day.

Table 7.2   Schiphol Airport: consolidated profit and loss (in 000s of
guilders)

	1988	1989	1990
Operating revenue			
Airport fees	210 365	218 482	242 881
Concessions	92 967	112 159	124 313
Catering	54 997	59 160	62 549
Rents and leases	55 672	58 319	65 331
Utility services	25 146	27 544	29 428
Other	57 537	73 527	89 885
Net turnover	496 684	549 191	614 387
Other	6 691	25 952	10 213
Total operating revenue	503 375	575 143	624 600
Operating expenditure			
Maintenance	39 542	41 265	38 778
Personnel	169 203	185 102	186 803
Depreciation	103 507	123 799	125 652
Other	136 627	156 784	183 820
Total operating expenditure	448 879	506 950	535 053
Operating result	54 496	68 193	89 547
Financial revenue and expenditure	8 553	15 508	23 526
Trading result	45 943	52 685	66 021
Taxation	998	102	98
Share from participations	114	321	2 010
Extraordinary expenditures		13 100*	
Result after taxes	44 831	52 904	54 964

Note:
* Provision for reorganisation costs.

addition to the airport fees, a major source of income is from the
concessions given for the operation of the duty-free shops. The
Schiphol management, which obtains a variable commission on all
sales through the shops, has been very careful to create a strictly-
controlled shopping centre with a world-wide reputation for quality,
service and low prices. Fourteen specialist shopkeepers, selected by
Schiphol management to ensure that there is no competition
between them, operate within the airport terminal selling at prices
determined by the airport management. These prices are established
in such a manner as to ensure the cheapest tax-free shopping centre

in Europe. In return, Schiphol provides promotional support in the form of advertising and such promotional material as the ubiquitous yellow shopping bags now synonymous with Amsterdam for travellers around the world. In maintaining such tight control, Schiphol has been able to create a single global identity and has avoided problems such as those encountered at other major European airports' duty-free shops where the owners, to compensate for the airport commission, increase their prices to a level equal to or sometimes higher than the prices found in city centres.

The remaining 41 per cent of the airport's income is derived from the leasing and rental of office space and facilities as well as utility services and catering. While the Schiphol Airport Authority has a fully-owned subsidiary operating as a caterer, it does not come into competition with the in-flight catering services of KLM, Trust-House Forte and Cuisinair, concentrating instead on providing restaurant service within the airport facilities themselves.

1989–91: A TURBULENT TAKE-OFF INTO THE 1990s

All predictions indicate a doubling of the volume of passenger and cargo traffic at Schiphol and other major international airports around the world in the next fifteen years. Yet, while this dramatic increase will undoubtedly take place, due in large part to the increased mobility of individuals and the accompanying globalisation of the world economy, the events that occurred between 1989 and the beginning of 1991 indicate that the expected growth may not be without some unfortunate surprises.

For example, 1989 proved disappointing for Schiphol as it came face to face with a saturated charter market. Many of Europe's summer holidaymakers travel on charter packages to such destinations as Palma (Majorca), Athens and Malaga. However, the present air system is unable to meet the increasing summer demand for air lanes by the charter companies, causing extensive delays throughout the European network (the punctuality of European carriers within Europe is worsening each year, due to particularly congested skies over Germany, France and Britain). Until additional military airspace is turned over to commercial use, this situation is not likely to change, thus putting an upper limit on the number of civil passengers that will be able to travel by air.

In early 1991, the world suffered political and economic uncertainty as war broke out in the Middle East. The war proved
short, at least on a global level, and life went back to 'business as
usual' by the time spring came around. However, as anxiety over
terrorist attacks mounted, the airlines saw their prime customers,
the business travellers, staying at home, communicating by fax and
telephone. While these downturns are usually transitory situations,
they are sufficient to make managers turn pale, particularly after
having approved expansion plans worth two billion dollars, as is the
case with Schiphol. This said, Schiphol's management is nevertheless expecting an increase in both its passenger and cargo traffic
(1–3 per cent and 2–4 per cent respectively for 1991).

SCHIPHOL MAINPORT: A POLICY OF 'CONTROLLED GROWTH' TO GEAR UP FOR THE YEAR 2000 AND BEYOND

The management of a private company whose objective is profit
and long-term survival is a complicated business, even in the most
favourable of circumstances. But, add such considerations as social
responsibility and civic duty, ecological concerns and national
interests as well as profits and long-term growth and you are faced
with a seemingly infinite amount of contradictory and often
insurmountable problems. This is, in many aspects, the situation
in which the Schiphol management finds itself.

The Netherlands has a long history of international trade with
countries throughout the world. The Dutch have a reputation for
being innovative, hard-working, aggressive businessmen who usually get what they want. But, in today's global economy, competition is tight and can come from the most unexpected areas. As a
result, the forces that have worked historically to secure a leading
position are no longer at play. In the case of The Netherlands, it is
well situated geographically, has a strong economy and currency,
boasts some of the world's leading multinationals, and is a tourist
centre, but it has a limited population. For Schiphol management,
this limited population is a major consideration and, perhaps, a
stumbling block for, if they are to obtain the status of a European
mainport, then they must in some way secure passenger and cargo
traffic of up to twice their present levels. This traffic must, by virtue

of the aforementioned circumstances, come from countries other than The Netherlands. Taking into consideration the fact that Schiphol has succeeded in extending its natural origin–destination market beyond its national borders, as well as the figures indicating Schiphol's passenger and cargo market shares relative to other leading European airports, it would seem fair to assume that such an objective, though ambitious and extremely expensive, should be feasible (see Tables 7.3 and 7.4).

If Schiphol Airport is to become a European mainport, what must be done? And what are the challenges to be faced? At present, Schiphol airport has an annual capacity of approximately 18 million passengers per year. Hence, with 16.5 million passengers, it is very close to its maximum capacity. The immediate objective is to

Table 7.3   Schiphol Airport: passenger market shares versus populations (in percentages)

Country	Passenger market shares N. Atlantic	Population
Belgium	4	5
Switzerland	5	3
The Netherlands	10	7
France	13	28
Germany	23	32
UK	45	25

Table 7.4   Schiphol Airport: freight (tonnage) market shares versus GNP (in percentages)

Country	Tonnage market shares N. Atlantic	GNP
Belgium	7	4
Switzerland	5	5
The Netherlands	15	7
France	18	27
Germany	21	33
UK	34	24

gradually increase capacity to 30 million passengers per year by the year 2003 and, looking further ahead to 2015, to 50 million. In addition, to maintain its European position as a leader, this passenger increase must be accompanied by an increase in cargo capacity. At present, the system limits cargo to 1 000 000 tonnes per year; by 2015, it is envisaged that it will have a capacity of 4 500 000 tonnes. This implies a dramatic increase in terminal and storage facility surface area as well as in the number of piers and gates for aircraft. These are risky though seemingly necessary projects if Schiphol is to attract the 'mega' carriers being produced as a result of deregulation.

Handling 30 million passengers per year is a feat of logistics that has implications for every functional aspect of the airport. If one travels through Schiphol today, the beginnings of these expansion projects are already visible. To begin with, two additional piers are being added to the existing four and one of the original piers is being extended to form a 'Y'. But plans do not stop here. A completely new terminal building is going to be added in parts. This terminal will be connected to the existing arrival and departure halls to maintain the airport's concept of 'everything under one roof'. Further along the time span, an additional pier will be built across the road that presently cuts through the airport area. This pier will have a capacity of twenty-three aircraft and will be connected to the main terminal building by a sophisticated automatic rail transport 'people mover'.

Yet the challenges of the future do not only lie in being able to ensure the capacity. Such an expansion must be accompanied by an efficient internal logistics system. Then and only then will airlines begin to be convinced that Schiphol is a better alternative to Brussels, London or Frankfurt. New roads will have to be built, car parking facilities extended, public transport mechanisms rendered even more sophisticated and efficient and, eventually, a new runway will be required if for no other reason than to provide flight paths that avoid congested residential areas. These kinds of plans cannot be decided upon in an internal meeting, but must be justified to the country, the municipalities and, perhaps most importantly, to the surrounding community residents who enjoy the privilege of being woken all through the night by 747s.

The population and government of The Netherlands are particularly concerned with ecological and environmental issues and therefore watch closely the expansion plans presently embarked upon by the Schiphol management. To justify itself, the management has used the argument that they are an organisation performing a function that is of national importance: they provide jobs (up to 73 000 could eventually be directly employed at the airport by the year 2015, while an additional 80 000 will have jobs related to airport functions, though off airport premises) and trade, the lifeblood of the Dutch economy. Thus far, the plans have been approved.

Now arises the issue of how to protect the surrounding area. Measures being introduced range from the definition of noise zones to the insulation of houses, at the expense of the airlines using Schiphol. One of the measures, the gradual phasing out of 'Chapter 2' aircraft,[3] may cause Schiphol to lose some business, particularly from airlines whose fleets consist of older aircraft long since discarded by the leading carriers. Such measures are part and parcel of the expense of planning for the future.

Turning attention away from the outside of the airport and the overall facilities, the next step is to look at the implications of expansion for the inside of the buildings. At first glance, one would not think of very much being added: perhaps more shops, more banks, more passport control points; but, other than that, little else. But this is not so: the ominous presence of 1992 and all it implies begins to rear its head and highlight some major points of confusion.

When borders disappear in 1993, an individual will be able to fly anywhere within the European Community without going through passport control. This necessarily implies that the majority of flights in and out of Amsterdam will pass from being international to being domestic. The result of this is a complete redefinition of the internal space. It also, and perhaps more importantly, means the loss of up to 50 per cent of duty-free income.

---

3. Chapter 2 aircraft, such as the DC-9, Boeings 727, 737-100 and 200, and 747-100 and 200 will gradually be phased out at Schiphol and other European airports; by 1 April 2002, they will all have disappeared. The oldest, noisiest Chapter 1 aircraft such as the Boeing 707s and 727s have already been banned from most European airports.

But will such measures really go through by the end of 1992? At the moment, the Schiphol management believes they will not. Countries are by nature hesitant to lose control over who crosses their borders and these concerns have been heightened by the Gulf crisis. As a result, the 'free movement of individuals' could very well be delayed for a few years. On the other hand, some European Community countries have tentatively agreed, with the signing of the Schengen Accord, to implement free borders earlier than the rest of the Community. Britain has not signed such an accord. In order to avoid such problems, the 'Schengen' airports have asked for the simultaneous implementation of the Accord and the subsequent free movement of individuals throughout the European community. Otherwise, should the Schengen Accord come into effect as it stands now, it will necessitate the creation of an entire zone just for UK flights: a significant portion of Schiphol business. In essence, Schiphol will have to adopt a flexible structure that will allow it gradually to phase out border control for European flights.

To solve the problem arising from the loss of duty-free income, more shops will have to be built on the public side of the airport, to create a 'shopping mall' concept open to passengers as well as the general public while, in the intercontinental wing, larger duty-free shops with more choice will be built. The solution lies in compensating the loss of margin with volume and new activities.

But the problems relating to the European Community do not stop here. Schiphol would like to strengthen its position as a transfer point for intercontinental passengers. To do so, the maximum amount of convenience and quality services must be provided for the passengers as well as the airlines. But will European legislation allow this?

Let us imagine the following scenario: a passenger is flying from New York to Rome via Amsterdam. The initial leg of the voyage, New York–Amsterdam, is an intercontinental flight and, upon arrival in Amsterdam, the passenger must go through passport control before continuing on the domestic portion of his trip. But where does his luggage go through Customs? Amsterdam or Rome? If the answer is Amsterdam, then the time the passenger spends on the ground there could as much as double. For the airport, this implies a reduced capacity: the more time the passenger is on the ground and in the airport, the more space he takes. For the passenger and the airlines, all the convenience of a smooth transfer disappears. On the other hand, if the luggage goes through Customs in Rome, then the passenger can minimise his time on the ground, having only to go through passport control before continuing on to his final destination, preferably after having stopped off at the duty-free shops. It is issues like these that the airport management must face to be able to plan on a long-term basis and that could determine the extent of success of the envisaged plans for the twenty-first century. Luckily for Schiphol, with respect to this specific issue, there is now more or less consent that the 'port of final destination' method will be applicable for luggage after 1992, so allowing for the transfer of baggage to connecting aircraft without going through customs at the port of entry.

But what of competition? Surely, the leading airports of Europe will not sit idly by and see their business drift slowly but surely to Amsterdam? The most threatening competition that immediately comes to mind is from London, Frankfurt and Paris. Paris is a threat in that the airports situated at Roissy are convenient, efficient, very modern, and, at the moment, still have ample capacity. London (whose airports suffer from a bad reputation world-wide) and Frankfurt, on the other hand, are at or near capacity, both on the ground and in the air,[4] so the threat does not seem excessive here. However, should airports such as Manchester, Copenhagen, Brussels or Zurich decide to invest in their infrastructure, they then could provide a credible threat and a run for Schiphol's money, as could possible new airports in Munich and Berlin.

Predicting the future is a gamble that cannot be avoided, particularly in a sector such as the transport service industry, which requires heavy investments that, once initiated, are difficult or impossible to reverse. Provided the world economy does not suffer a prolonged and unpredicted number of shocks such as the Gulf Crisis, then all indications tend to make one believe that travel will be a booming business for decades to come. If so, then Schiphol

---

4. While airspace is limited over Europe at present, it is expected to increase in the years to come, because of two factors: new technology and the handing-over of military airspace for commercial use. Military airspace at present accounts for over half of European airspace.

Schiphol Airport's Master Plan 2003

Phase I: 1989–93

(Total budget: 1.7 billion guilders)
The first phase of the development project includes:

- initial terminal building extension;
- increase in baggage handling capacity;
- construction of a fifth pier (E); and
- modernisation and extension of central road system, including the building of more car-parking spaces.

Phase II: 1994–98

During this five-year period, the Schiphol management hopes to complete the following projects:

- second extension of the terminal building;
- two-way flight path approach to increase flight frequency;
- construction of a sixth pier and the second 'fork' extension to pier B;
- construction of automatic rail passenger transport system ('people mover') between the central terminal building and the projected sixth pier;
- construction of a new cargo area; and
- further modernisation of the central road system.

Phase III: 1999–2003

The projects foreseen for the third phase will only be realised should traffic needs demand them. They include:

- third and final expansion of the terminal building;
- further expansion of the cargo facilities;
- expansion of the 'people mover' network; and
- construction of a further pier

airport has every chance of suceeding in becoming a European mainport. The necessary infrastructure is in place and being expanded (to include eventually direct access to the planned Paris–Amsterdam high-speed train, the TGV (Très Grande Vitesse), as well as the Amsterdam–Cologne high speed service), the airport is known and well regarded world-wide;[5] and the airlines are already using the airport. The future lies in quality and service and it is in this that the Schiphol management wants to excel. If the passengers are satisfied, and the costs of operating there are reasonable, then the airlines will continue to want to use Schiphol. Eventually, some airlines other than KLM could want to make it a major European hub. This is particularly applicable if only five or six European airports survive as mainports, reducing the rest to feeder 'regioports'.

---

5. Together with Singapore Airport, Schiphol is consistently rated by passengers as one of the world's best. Interestingly, the team responsible for the Singapore Airport is the same one that created Schiphol in its present form.

8 SAS Scandinavian Airlines: Strategic Alliances in the Making

> There are clear limitations to how far we can develop and refine the specific air transport product . . . We have to identify and evaluate the business traveller's total service needs. In the 1980s we saw a customer in every individual. In the 1990s, we see an individual in every customer . . . Our strategy is to distribute traffic to as many important destinations as possible in a global system, offering non-stop or at the most one-stop service in co-ordination with our partners . . . .
>
> (Jan Carlzon, President and Chief Executive Officer, the SAS Group)

Among those in the travel industry, and more specifically air travel, the mere mention of SAS Scandinavian Airlines brings forth comments of envy and admiration as well as fear. Consistently rated as one of the world's best airlines in terms of safety, punctuality and service, it has proved to be one of Europe's most successful and competitively aggressive airlines, with a knack not only for survival but also for profitability in the face of hard times. This has been the case since 1981, when Jan Carlzon was named Chief Operating Officer of the Group (after entering in 1980 as Chief Executive Officer of SAS) and began the now-legendary turnaround of a company then in financial trouble.

Yet it seems clear that with the beginning of the 1990s, a new wave of problems are setting in, not only for SAS, but for the European air industry as a whole: a fragmented industry is about to be hit with deregulation and the uncertain consequences that accompany such a phenomenon. Operating from the edge of the European continent and with a population base of only 17 million people, SAS sees the proposed deregulation as both an opportunity and a threat, one which Carlzon believes can only be confronted through the creation of strong strategic alliances around the world. The alliances, either in the making or in a phase of consolidation, constitute the core of SAS's strategy for the 1990s.

THE INITIAL TURNAROUND

Prior to the 1973 oil crisis, the world's airlines had operated in a supplier's market: with demand far in excess of supply, the airline industry grew fat and lazy, hiring excess staff and building up fleets based more on prestige than on necessity. In 1973, the oil crisis brought to light just how inefficient many airlines had grown, thus initiating broad and often haphazard cost-cutting based more on the short-term rather than the long-term consequences. Assuming that price and product were fixed, the airlines saw the only variable as being costs. Disregarding market demands and preferences, airlines cut costs equally across all areas, often eliminating their respective competitive advantages and resulting in unmotivated staff and unsatisfied clients.[1] SAS was no exception.

Over 1979 and 1980, SAS had an accumulated loss of approximately 30 million dollars, this after a record seventeen years of profit. Aware that action needed to be taken, the SAS Board offered Carlzon, then President of Linjeflyg, Sweden's domestic airline, the chance to initiate a turnaround process that would counter the losses and put SAS once again in a healthy situation. The popular assumption was that Carlzon would implement strategies similar to those he had carried out in the past, both at Linjeflyg and at Vingresor, the tour operator: cut prices and squeeze costs. However, SAS proved to be in a situation where neither option could work. Costs had already been cut as much as was feasible and the lowering of fares would only have initiated international price wars, an alternative most detrimental to SAS itself. Instead, Carlzon introduced a high-risk, aggressive approach to conquer the most profitable segment of the market, the business traveller, by offering the best possible service in the market. The proposed strategy was subsequently and enthusiastically accepted.

With a total investment of 25 million dollars and an increase in operating expenses nearing 12 million dollars, Carlzon's aim was to increase earnings by 115 million dollars over a three-year period; much to everyone's surprise, 80 million dollars of this target was achieved in the first year alone.

---

1. See Jan Carlzon, *Moments of Truth* (New York: Harper & Row, 1989).

The success of the approach centres on Carlzon having decided to focus on the needs of the business traveller, using SAS's expenditure as an asset aimed at offering the best, rather than as a liability, and then cutting all expenditure for services regarded as unimportant.[2] In short, costs were reallocated to where they were visible. EuroClass was created, providing check-in facilities, airport lounges and upgraded in-flight service for the executive at the price of a full-fare economy ticket, against the competition, who practised a policy of charging a premium for these extra services.

However, the visible exterior changes had to have corresponding interior changes if the strategy was to succeed. Taking SAS's highly centralised and top-heavy structure, Carlzon proceeded to introduce a totally decentralised decision-making process, thus delegating responsibility to those who were on the 'front line': the thousands of SAS employees who come into contact with passengers. With new uniforms on the outside to accompany and confirm the new mentality on the inside and, simultaneously, life with the unions became more co-operative, as it was now difficult for the unions to reject what the employees themselves saw as being in their own interests. In fact, much of the success of the dramatic turnaround effort begun in 1980 is due to Carlzon's basic premises and beliefs regarding management and leadership:

> The challenge is to make the unions your partner in establishing the overall direction of the company. (Jan Carlzon to the American Management Association, 20 April 1988)

> A leader is not appointed because he knows everything and can make every decision. He is appointed to bring together the knowledge that is available and then create the prerequisites for the work to be done. He creates the systems that enable him to delegate responsibility for day-to-day operations. (Jan Carlzon, *Moments of Truth*)

---

2. While increasing expenses by 45 million dollars, a programme called TRIM was initiated to cut other expenses by 40 million dollars. Among the measures taken was the abolition of almost all paperwork and manuals so as to unblock the top-heavy system that existed thus far. Starting from scratch, only the necessary formalities were reintroduced.

Had the employees of SAS not been told that they could make mistakes, and were actually encouraged to do so, without the risk of losing their jobs, the unorthodox initiatives would undoubtedly not have met with the success they did. While mistakes did occur, the heightened sense of corporate identity as well as the knowledge of where the company was going and why, far outweighed any negative results. On the other hand, the delegation of authority to where the customer was did have important implications for middle management: they suddenly found themselves being circumvented. Employees no longer respected the traditional chains of command, instead addressing their problems and inquiries directly to senior management. Middle managers found their base of authority disappearing, but saw little with which to replace it. With SAS once again on relatively solid ground, Carlzon and his staff have now begun the process of rectifying this situation by training middle managers to become to their staff what Carlzon is to SAS: a visionary, guide and leader.

Despite the anger of competitors such as Air France and British Airways, who saw SAS's rapidly-increasing market share, Carlzon steamed on, constantly aiming to perfect service both on the ground and in the air. Yet, even with the success achieved, such a strategy was not enough to sustain a strong position through the 1990s as it had in the 1980s. With intense competition coming from Asia's low cost carriers and the United States' mega-carriers as well as Europe's more centrally-situated airlines, the SAS Board recognised the need to find a more solid base that, in the face of deregulation, would guarantee profitable survival and would not cause SAS to become merely a feeder carrier for the likes of Lufthansa and British Airways.

THE CHALLENGE OF A DEREGULATED EUROPE

The skies of Europe are in the process of undergoing deep and irreversible changes as the European Community staggers or races, depending on one's perspective, towards the creation of a deregulated market. With European airlines hitherto protected by a system of bilateral government agreements for the operation of commercial flights, the European Community aims to increase competition, and hence improve quality and provide lower prices to the consumer, by introducing legislation that will in theory permit more flexible airfares, greater freedom in capacity and market entry, and will promote links between major centres and regional airports. While the goals may appear noble at first glance, the actual implementation is proving to be a bureaucratic headache for all concerned in the air travel industry. Political preferences and a lack of understanding on the part of Community decision-makers of the needs of either the consumer or the air carriers, are causing fear of greater control of the industry rather than less. This has been the situation since 1987, when the European Community ruled that aviation was subject to legislation on competition and hence to effective control by the Commission. This being the case, the objective of all airlines has been and continues to be to gain the most influence possible within the EC, a challenge obviously more attainable for the state-held mega-carriers such as Air France or, until recently, British Airways.

In promoting deregulation, the EC has used the United States as an example to establish guidelines. This is perhaps the EC's first big mistake with respect to European air travel. To begin with, and subsequent to the deregulation of the American market in the 1970s, the top five American airlines now control 80 per cent of the market. This situation is diametrically opposed to the one being faced in Europe, where the industry is characterised by a high degree of fragmentation due to the number of countries operating airlines. Secondly, flights in the United States are, on average, long-haul flights, while a majority of European flights are of under two hours' duration; this implies that the American concept of 'hubbing'[3] is more difficult to implement in Europe, often forcing companies to operate unprofitable but necessary routes. Thirdly, competition in the United States is based on city-pairs, of which there are over twenty-five, handling more than a million passengers

---

3. 'Hubbing' consists of using an airport as a major transfer point to connect from long-haul flights to regional flights, or between regional flights. As an example, Continental Airlines and SAS use Newark, NJ, as a hub to provide one-stop service between Europe and more than fifty United States' destinations. The advantage of hubbing is the increased number of connections, while the disadvantage is the loss of non-stop potential.

per year (a city-pair is simply the name attributed to an air route linking two cities, without a stopover). Europe boasts only six, four of which are domestic routes. The EC is stipulating that there must be more than two carriers on each city pair, as in the United States, despite European traffic not being heavy enough. Furthermore, according to the EC, it is the dominant carrier, that is, the one whose home country it is, which must cede airport slots to a new entrant. So, while on the one hand the EC is promoting open competition, on the other it is attempting to control aircraft and route licensing, without having really studied the market situation. To add to the general confusion, the EC is aiming to remove the existing distinctions between regularly-scheduled air traffic and charter services, the latter accounting for 60 per cent of European air travel.

In the United States, deregulation has created a situation of 'buy-and-sell' of airport slots, gates and routes among the airlines, but the issues are becoming increasingly politicised on the other side of the Atlantic. This is particularly true as national carriers scramble to safeguard their relative positions before the EC produces a definitive statement on aviation competition policy.

Turning more specifically to the position of the Scandinavian countries and SAS, the situation becomes obscured in a bank of administrative Community fog. Because SAS is partly Danish,[4] the EC has ruled that it is subject to Community aviation laws. Taking into consideration the relatively small size of Denmark when compared to the likes of France, Germany and the United Kingdom, the Danish Government has found itself in a poor negotiating position, prompting it to require that Norway and Sweden be

---

4. SAS is a consortium of Danish Airlines, Norwegian Airlines and Swedish Airlines. Each of the three parent companies is owned 50 per cent by private interests and 50 per cent by government shareholders in each of the respective countries. In the consortium, Danish and Norwegian Airlines own two-sevenths each and Swedish Airlines own three-sevenths. The shares of the three parent companies are traded on the stock exchanges of Copenhagen, Oslo and Stockholm. SAS does not receive subsidies from any of its governments. Furthermore, SAS is entirely free to borrow whatever funds are required to further the interests of the airline without regard to any governmental or share-holder approval.

included in all EC[5] matters relating to aviation. This stipulation has in turn led to an agreement, signed in March 1991, defining Norway and Sweden as Community member states with respect to aviation issues and thus subject to Community laws. This implies that SAS will soon find itself competing against more foreign carriers within its native Scandinavian market.

For the SAS Group, being responsible to private as well as government shareholders is complicated by the fact that, in Sweden and Norway, negotiations regarding aviation must include the Ministries of Transport and Foreign Affairs and the Civil Aviation Authorities. The EC is now added to the list.

LOOKING FOR PARTNERS

While it is clear that the United States' experience with air travel deregulation cannot be directly compared to the present European situation, there are nevertheless some valuable lessons to be learned:

- The first has been the emergence of 'hub and spoke' systems, created by the major carriers in an effort to broaden market and network coverage and create more efficient connection patterns.
- The second is the brutal price wars initiated by all the carriers in the hopes of gaining market share. These price wars have caused massive industry restructuring through extensive cost-cutting, repeated mergers and acquisitions, and bankruptcies, as witnessed in the recent examples of Eastern Airlines, America West, Pan Am and TWA, though the latter has thus far avoided 'Chapter 11' (a US legal measure that allows bankrupt companies to restructure). The most successful of the American carriers have been Delta Airlines and American Airlines, both of which have coupled an aggressive expansion and fare policy with service upgrading.
- The third major effect has been the creation of biased distribution systems by the successful airlines as a means of capturing

---

5. Denmark has asked that all EFTA (European Free Trade Association) countries be included in talks. This is, however, unlikely, as the EC will probably link such an agreement to other, non-related, issues.

the market and eliminating the competition. While legislation has since been introduced in both the United States and Europe to prevent such biases, these systems initially functioned in such a way that, when travel agents called up information on their computers, the airline whose system it was showed its flights ahead of all competitors. Many believe that it is such a system, developed by American Airlines and widely distributed throughout the United States, that effectively ruined People Express, the low-cost, no-frills airline. Through its system, American Airlines was able to match and beat all fares offered by People Express; because of American's size, network and reputed service, it became virtually impossible for People Express to survive in the long run, particularly as it did not have its own system.

With the prospect of fare alterations in Europe as well as the arrival of numerous new airlines such as Air Europe,[6] SAS has been seeking ways to emulate the American 'hub and spoke' system by forming strategic partnerships on a global as opposed to a European scale and thus secure traffic through a sophisticated network. Jan Carlzon sees this as an essential part of the airline's strategy for the 1990s, as SAS is at present unable to become a mega-carrier on a par with Europe's three major airlines: British Airways, Air France and Lufthansa. As mentioned earlier, SAS has multiple disadvantages stemming from its peripheral geographic location and small market base as well as its high cost of operations due to Scandinavia's exorbitant social expenses. Furthermore, and partly as a result of the former of these factors, SAS has traditionally been weak on the long-haul routes.[7]

---

6. Air Europe, a recent arrival among European air carriers, succeeded in capturing 15 per cent of SAS's and British Airways' market share in tourist class between Scandinavia and the UK by providing lower fares, made possible by substantially lower overhead costs. However, Air Europe declared bankruptcy in 1991.

7. At present, 80 per cent of SAS's traffic is derived from European and domestic traffic and 20 per cent from intercontinental flights, the latter being quite low when compared to an airline such as Holland's KLM, whose intercontinental traffic accounts for over 90 per cent of its income.

SAS's weakness on intercontinental routes is perhaps best reflected in its lack of destinations within the United States, particularly when compared to KLM or British Airways, who serve up to fifteen or more cities each, as against SAS's four. Unable to get American approval to increase the number of gates, despite significant lobbying efforts, Carlzon and his team have focused instead on ways round the legal barriers, which they have found in an alliance with Continental Airlines.

The search for an American partner proved to be long and arduous. The most important factor for SAS was to strike an agreement with an airline which has a well-developed domestic network into which SAS could efficiently feed its Scandinavian passengers. Furthermore, the airline in question would ideally be based in the New York area, SAS's main US entry point. There were, in fact, few airlines meeting such requirements. PanAm seemed eager to strike up an agreement with anyone willing to inject cash into its deteriorating balance sheet, but it lacked the necessary domestic routes. Then Continental Airlines appeared.

Continental, operating out of New Jersey from Newark's new third terminal and with over sixty domestic destinations, seemed a possible candidate despite certain problems, the primary one being that it was held by Frank Lorenzo's Texas Air Group, which included the now defunct Eastern Airlines. Frank Lorenzo has gained the reputation of being a difficult negotiator and has the illustrious characteristic of being despised by all trade unions. Symbolised by his dramatic cost-cutting strategies, primarily on Eastern Airlines, he has fought the unions on every front, to the point of actively hiring only non-union personnel. But his strategy has resulted in several strikes which were ultimately responsible for the demise of Eastern Airlines.

In 1988, SAS bought 9.9 per cent of the Texas Air Group. Since those negotiations, when SAS saw itself being criticised and black-listed by the American unions for even dealing with Lorenzo, SAS has managed to oust him from control of Continental by buying him out. Today, the SAS Group is the single largest shareholder in Continental Airlines, with a stake of 16.8 per cent.

The results of the alliance have proved extremely rewarding. By transferring all SAS's services from New York's J. F. Kennedy International Airport to Continental's terminal at Newark International Airport, situated just across the river, SAS has managed to increase transfer traffic by 60 per cent in the first full year alone (1989), thus regaining the Scandinavia–United States traffic that had previously been lost to competing European carriers offering direct service out of London and Amsterdam. With the two airlines providing for through-check-in from Scandinavia to anywhere in the US and vice versa, as well as easy transfer procedures in Newark, passengers now have daily one-stop service from Oslo, Copenhagen and Stockholm to over sixty American cities.

Shortly after SAS made its second investment in Continental Airlines, increasing its stake from 9.9 per cent to 16.8 per cent, Continental went into 'Chapter 11' protection from its creditors. The airline is now in a restructuring process, while benefiting from motivated staff as well as extensive service training for all of its 25 000 front line employees at the joint Continental/SAS Quality Service Institute recently created in Houston, Texas.

Compared to the United States, South-East Asia and the Far East have proved to be much less of a challenge for SAS's expansion strategy. Until the mid-1970s, SAS had a 30 per cent stake in Thailand's Thai International for which it provided extensive technical and commercial support. Thus it seemed that Thai would be a natural partner with which to cover the South-East Asian market. Also, part of Thai's undeniable attractiveness is its reputation for high-quality service, a network including seventy cities worldwide and its healthy balance sheet.

Today, SAS and Thai have concentrated services between Scandinavia and Bangkok, providing twice-daily non-stop service from either Copenhagen or Stockholm. With this service in place, Thai is now aiming to improve its feeder service for through connections to other Asian cities.

In the Far East, All Nippon Airways (ANA), the world's eighth largest airline,[8] presented itself to SAS as a partner candidate in an effort to expand its network beyond its essentially domestic Japanese route system. With ANA's extensive operations, including travel agencies, tour operators, catering and hotel businesses, wholesale and retail trading and a 3.5 per cent stake in Austrian

---

8. ANA is the world's eighth largest airline in terms of passengers carried (27.5 million in 1989).

Airlines, SAS has gained a solid foothold in the Japanese and Far Eastern markets through the alliance formed. Though still to be further developed, the deal struck has succeeded in increasing connections between Tokyo and Scandinavia, with SAS and ANA operating joint flights on SAS aircraft.[9]

Turning to South America, the situation has proven to be more complex and volatile. South America is characterised by political instability on the one hand and a lack of attractive potential partners on the other, with the possible exception of Brazil's Varig. In addition, South America is not an essential market for Scandinavia, the traffic between the two areas being quite limited.

When initial talks with Varig failed, SAS turned to the next most attractive prospect: Aerolineas Argentinas. Negotiations began, but SAS's offer expired before legislation authorising the deal could pass through Congress. The search for a South-American partner was temporarily suspended until, during negotiations in 1988 with Frank Lorenzo in New York, Carlzon and his team were approached by a Chilean investor to strike a deal with LanChile, the Chilean national carrier. Unwilling to get involved in Chile's internal political problems, with the possible complications this could entail at home when facing the unions and the three governments, SAS at first rejected the investment offer. However, the option was reconsidered when it became apparent that the Chilean Government was making efforts to put in place a democratic system. SAS subsequently acquired a 35 per cent stake in LanChile.

Of all the partnership deals SAS is now involved in, the investment in LanChile appears to be the one with the most question marks attached to it. LanChile, operating out of Santiago, is a small carrier with a limited market and a small fleet of planes, despite unused traffic rights from South America to Europe and North America. Furthermore, SAS's and LanChile's routes do not match up in that SAS only flies to São Paolo, Brazil, a point from which LanChile has a quite limited service, though it does connect with SAS.

---

9. On the Stockholm–Tokyo routes, the airlines use an SAS Boeing 767 with SAS pilots and a mixed SAS/ANA cabin crew. SAS and ANA share all expenses and profits on a 50/50 basis.

With most of the globe covered through an extensive network of international hubs, SAS can now offer direct or one-stop service from Scandinavia to anywhere in the world. The only part missing from this jigsaw puzzle was Europe itself: if SAS were to survive through to the end of the century as a major actor in European and world commercial aviation, it would need to secure a solid home base, protected as much as possible from the dominant European carriers. To do so would require economies of scale, negotiating power and a comprehensive European network.

The search for a partner in Europe proved to be more complicated and more politically influenced than any of the negotiations encountered elsewhere. While the European Community aims to create a single market, the reality of the business environment only emphasises how much the issue of national pride dominates and the extent to which national governments are willing to protect their own companies' interests, even if it means subsidising an unprofitable business. This is particularly true in the case of national air carriers, whose very existence appear to symbolise a nation's prestige and importance to both governments and citizens. This is nowhere more poignantly displayed than in Belgium, ironically the seat of government for the European Community.

SAS saw Brussels as a potentially important hub right in the heart of Europe. Situated between the congested airports of London, Amsterdam and Frankfurt, Brussels offered not only a central location, but an under-utilised airport and good prospects for future growth. To establish links there implied creating an alliance with Sabena, Belgium's national carrier and for many years the target of travellers' disparaging jokes because of its comparatively bad service both in the air and on the ground, be it abroad or at Brussels airport, now much in need of modernisation.

SAS approached Sabena in 1986 to discuss the possibility of merging the two companies; however, talks broke down when both sides realised they were unable to make such a dramatic move. Also recognising the advantages of a Brussels hub, British Airways and KLM later made a joint offer of acquisition. The Belgian Government approved the British Airways/KLM deal; they were, however, blocked by the Belgian courts as well as the EC since the deal was seen as leading to a potential abuse of a future, dominant market position. In light of this situation, the Belgian government chose instead to subsidise Sabena. Today, Sabena is undergoing extensive restructuring with the help of massive but legally questionable (under EC competition laws) government subsidies (in the order of US$1.5 billion) while British Airways, on its side, has filed a letter of intent to buy.

With the outlook in Belgium being somewhat bleak, in 1987, Jan Carlzon decided to strike on SAS's arch rival's home ground by going after British Airways' leading national competitor, British Caledonian Airways (BCal). But SAS's acquisition bid was not to succeed, even though it was conducted under the umbrella of Prime Minister Margaret Thatcher's supposedly more liberal business environment. With the prospect of a foreign carrier obtaining control of a leading British airline, British Airways, which had already made a bid for BCal, stepped in to block SAS's proposal lodged with the British Government and subsequently made a counter-offer. Both bids were held up by government procedures and endless debates on the legality of SAS's move. When the government finally gave approval for SAS to go ahead, the buying price had gone from SAS's original offer of £120 million for 25 per cent (the maximum allowed for a foreign carrier) to £250 million for a 100 per cent buy-out, thus representing a considerable decrease in the valuation of BCal by British Airways. Deciding nevertheless that the price was too high, SAS opened the way for BCal's acquisition by British Airways, but this left SAS still without a European partner.

SAS's management switched gears and looked instead to the privately-held airlines of Britain Holdings plc (ABH), the second-largest airline group in the United Kingdom and the owners of Manx Airlines, Loganair, London City Airways and British Midland, the only other British carrier allowed to operate international flights from Heathrow. Eager to expand internationally, the holding welcomed SAS's offer to buy 24.9 per cent of its shares. Primarily domestic, British Midland and its sister companies now offer SAS passengers an extensive network within the British Isles.

SAS had now managed to strike directly at British Airways; but this was not enough to solidify its position in continental Europe. As a result, Jan Carlzon conducted parallel negotiations with Swissair and together they eventually formed the European Quality Alliance (EQA), an organisation that is expected to provide wide cost savings, improved passenger service and a broader market base throughout the 1990s. Austrian Airlines and Finnair have also joined the EQA.

THE EUROPEAN QUALITY ALLIANCE

SAS and Swissair[10] had commercial ties during the 1950s and 1960s, but neither had done much to actually tighten the bond. With the approach of 1993, both sides have realised that a co-operation agreement can only be beneficial; however, when the negotiating process began, Jan Carlzon wanted more than just a piece of paper, as appeared to be the case between Air France and Lufthansa.[11] As a result, it was finally agreed that a limited amount of cross-ownership would be part of the deal.[12] The specific reasoning behind the creation of the European Quality Alliance can essentially be analysed from two perspectives: from the market and from the production sides.

From a market point of view, the concept is relatively straightforward in that the objective is simply to create a joint traffic system in such a way as to maximise the number of destinations and improve ease of travel for the passenger. This involves adjusting timetables to improve connections and providing through-check-in, that is, the passenger receives boarding passes and seating for the entire trip at the point of departure, even if a change of aircraft is scheduled. In addition, the two airlines aim to provide a globally-integrated travel service.

In the future, improved service will also include guaranteeing endorsable airfares. While this is commonplace today, airlines are becoming increasingly possessive towards passengers and are constantly thinking up new ways to hold them. One option

---

10. Swissair, the Swiss flag carrier, is 23 per cent government-owned. In addition, the Swissair group owns 51 per cent of the Swiss regional airline Crossair as well as 5 per cent of the United States' Delta Airlines and 10 per cent of Austrian Airlines, not to mention two Swiss charter carriers, Balair and CTA.

11. In 1990, Air France and Lufthansa announced publicly that they would continue to co-operate with each other in agreeing routes and fares. However, as it was designed more to scare the competition, the agreement has little substance behind it.

12. The level of cross-ownership will be 7.5 per cent of total shares on either side. Both SAS and Swissair are in the process of deciding the details of the transaction, that is, when the respective shares should be bought.

envisaged is the creation of non-endorsable (that is, non-transferable) airfares, even for those travelling Business Class or First Class.

From a production point of view, the ultimate objective is to improve efficiency and lower costs. SAS's principal problem is its extremely high cost of operations. In a major effort to become competitive with the Asian carriers as well as some of the leading European carriers, SAS has introduced a restructuring programme, aimed at increasing productivity by 20 per cent, which by 1993 will have eliminated 3500 jobs and reduced the overall annual cost level by 3 billion Swedish krone (approximately 16 per cent of operating costs). SAS's present situation is aggravated by the fact that, unlike other European carriers, it cannot receive government subsidies, but only new share capital, thus creating a situation which is extremely favourable for the likes of Air France, Alitalia and Sabena.[13] However, the EC is expected to ban such subsidies in the near future.

It is no wonder, then, that the EQA is seen as having great potential. Swissair, Austrian Airlines, Finnair and SAS have begun reviewing all areas of operation to examine where synergies can be obtained. A number of priorities have been established regarding both market and production synergies.

One such priority is in the area of station services, where the joining of ground personnel will help reduce expenses by avoiding duplication. Co-operation at this level is carried out in thirty airports, with an additional ten under study, and ranges from the mere sharing of services to one carrier taking full responsibility for the other.

Another priority lies in the area of data systems. SAS and Swissair are studying the possibility of creating a joint data company with the goal of developing, maintaining and operating data applications. Such an endeavour is complex in that it requires the airlines to agree on the same operations procedures and hence on their overall strategies. If accomplished, Austrian Airlines and Finnair may join at a later date. With four carriers now making up

---

13. Both Air France and Sabena received large government subsidies in 1991. In addition, British Airways, though now private, had the equivalent of $1 billion-worth of debt written off by the British Government prior to the company's privatisation.

the EQA, the cost savings through economies of scale in this area are potentially significant.[14]

The third priority involves fleet planning. When an airline orders an aircraft, it specifies all its characteristics, including the general layout of the plane and, as far as possible, the types of computers on the flight deck. This being the case, it is possible to have pilots flying an aircraft for one company who are unable to fly the same type belonging to another carrier. In order to avoid this, the four airlines of the EQA are working jointly to develop similar specifications and thus create the possibility of exchanging flight-deck crews.[15] Whether or not the four airlines will eventually have similar fleets is unclear. For now, the choice of the actual aircraft type remains in the hands of the individual company (see Tables 8.1 and 8.2).

Table 8.1   SAS Scandinavian Airlines: fleet, as of 31.12.89

Aircraft	SAS owned	SAS leased	SAS total	SAS on order	Swissair***
Boeing 767	5	–	5	11	–
Douglas DC10*	4	4	8	–	10
Douglas MD series 80**	35	–	35	34	22
Douglas DC9	46	14	60	–	–
Fokker F-27	5	–	5	–	–
Fokker F-50	6	–	6	16	–
Boeing 747	–	–	–	–	5
Airbus 310	–	–	–	–	9
Fokker 100	–	–	–	–	8
Total	101	18	119	61	54

Notes:
* As of 1991, the SAS fleet of DC10s had been completely replaced by the more efficient Boeing 767.
** The MD series 80 is an updated version of the DC9.
*** Finnair's fleet of 46 aircraft includes the DC10, Airbus 300, MD series 80, ATR 42, Saab 340 and Boeing 737.

---

14.   Swissair has a 10 per cent stake in Austrian Airlines. SAS was offered shares in Austrian, but it deemed the price to be too high.
15.   An advantage of such a system can already be seen: SAS at present has an extra 100 pilots on loan to Swissair.

Table 8.2 SAS Scandinavian Airlines: passenger, freight and mail traffic, 1989

	Passenger km	Cabin factor (percentages)	Freight (tonne/km)	Mail (tonne/km)
Intercontinental	6 787	74.1	376.7	34
Europe	5 290	56.6	31.4	16.1
Domestic	3 152	65.5	15	7.3
Total network	15 229	65.3	423.1	57.4

SAS has, in fact, invested close to US$5 billion in new aircraft, having chosen to replace the older, less efficient and high capacity fleet of McDonnell DC-10s with the new, extended range twin-engine Boeing 767. In addition to a significantly lower fuel consumption level when compared to the DC-10, the 767 has the added advantage of being a smaller aircraft more suitable to the needs of SAS (for instance, the aircraft's weight is considerably lower than that of the DC-10, meaning lower en-route charges and smaller landing fees).

The European Quality Alliance aims to provide advantages not only for the four airlines concerned, but also for their millions of passengers. Already well under way, it forms an integral part of SAS's strategy for the 1990s, as Jan Carlzon believes that such an association will, in addition to providing one of the world's largest international 'hub and spoke' route systems, provide the much-needed economies of scale for SAS to compete with the world's mega-carriers.

CREATING A GLOBAL TRAVEL GROUP

However, the strategy being implemented to ensure the profitable survival of SAS Scandinavian Airlines extends far beyond the airline itself. Convinced that the battleground of the future is not in the air, but on the ground, Jan Carlzon and his team are working on creating one of the world's largest travel service networks, to be able to offer to the group's clients the best and most comprehensive service possible, extending from a total travel service for the business traveller, including credit card services, tour packages and retailing (see Tables 8.3 and 8.4).

Perhaps the most aggressive and high-risk venture has been SAS's US$500 million investment in InterContinental hotels. Originally part of the PanAm Group, it was subsequently sold to Britain's Grand Metropolitan Group. Despite, or because of, drastic cost-cutting, the chain suffered poor performance levels under the management of Grand Metropolitan and was sold yet again to the Tsutsumi family of Japan. When contact with the Tsutsumi family was first established, the SAS Board remained very sceptical about the feasibility of such a deal, particularly because of the scope of the investment and its implications for the group as a whole: while obviously providing a chance to accelerate the expansion of SAS's hotel network, it also meant forsaking other investments for that year (1989). After initial discussions in Tokyo, Jan Carlzon and his colleagues returned to Stockholm highly enthusiastic, convinced that the Tsutsumis' Saison Group and the SAS Group shared the same philosophy with respect to the hotel group's future growth. Upon their return, they then had to convince the Board, a feat which consisted of constant flying between Stockholm, Oslo and Copenhagen to reassure the Board that they were embarking on a sound business venture. The Board finally approved, on condition that the financing of the project be done totally from within SAS's own hotel business unit.

Today, SAS clients have instant access to approximately 130 hotels world-wide and the Group is working on installing hotel check-in for EuroClass passengers, as well as other traditional SAS services, in as many of these as possible. The potential gains of such a network are perhaps best epitomised in the case of Brussels, where SAS has seen a 60 per cent increase in its business since the opening of its hotel there. In Jan Carlzon's own words:

Building up our own hotel chain to encompass all of the important destinations for business travellers would have taken a long time and required major financial and human resources. Instead we added 106 first class hotels in a single sweep . . . In their most sophisticated form, the hotels will take care of many tasks which traditionally are handled at the airports. (From the *1989 Annual Report*)

Table 8.3 The SAS Group business units

Business unit	Area of operations	Comments
SAS Airline	Domestic and international scheduled air traffic operations	
SAS International Hotels	Hotel operations and development	Includes 27 hotels and 40% of Intercontinental Hotels
SAS Service Partner	Catering and restaurants	Europe's largest flight catering service
SAS Trading	Wholesaling, retailing, mail order and media	1988 sales of US$200 million
SAS Leisure	Holiday packages, charter operations, resort hotels	Includes Vingresor, Sunwing, Scanair and Spanair
SAS Financial Services	Provides financial services and advice to the Group's other business units	Includes SAS Finance, Polygon Insurance, Aviation Holdings
Diners' Club Nordic	Credit cards and SAS cards	

Table 8.4   SAS Group: income per business unit (MSEK)*

Business unit	1990	1989	1988
SAS Airline	1 213	1 026	1 459
SAS International Hotels	−91	103	59
SAS Service Partner	190	211	184
SAS Trading	122	114	90
SAS Leisure	+2	−8	−6
SAS Financial Services**	+144	84	71

* Income = earnings before tax and extraordinary items.
** Due primarily to Diners' Club card service.

Carlzon has opted for an aggressive growth strategy via the formation of a global network of alliances and partnerships. With the advantage of having an airline recognised among international travellers as being one of the world's best in terms of both punctuality and service, not to mention safety, such a strategy stands a good chance of success. There is no doubt that the alliances have recaptured much of the traffic that had previously been lost to the likes of KLM and Lufthansa and that the potential economies of scale are enormous, particularly in the case of the European Quality Alliance and Continental Airlines. Yet there are certain key issues that will continue to weigh heavily until they are resolved or at least brought under control.

The first of these is, as already mentioned, the high operating costs. Scandinavia's high standard of living has come about as the result of tax rates as high as 80–90 per cent and at the expense of corporate efficiency. SAS has set ambitious objectives for improvements in efficiency (5 per cent per year for five years), but has so far been unable to meet all of them due to an inability to reduce costs as well as to recent slumps in the air travel industry. Many companies have, in fact, moved headquarters out of Scandinavia for this very reason, as is the case with Tetra-Pak and Ikea, now located in Switzerland. However, this would not appear to be a feasible alternative for the SAS Group.

Secondly, the SAS Group's expansion has necessitated large investments, the return on which could take longer than expected to come through.

Thirdly, the decentralisation of decision-making has created a question mark on the exact duties and responsibilities of middle management. While middle managers can be viewed as coaches for their staff, the issue then arises of whether they are prepared to eventually move up to senior positions.

Finally, until the European Community moves to enforce a definitive competition policy for the aviation industry, SAS is facing competitors who are able to solicit huge government subsidies as they prepare for the period of total deregulation. Brussels until now has not declared these subsidies to be either legal or illegal, thus allowing for rampant abuse of a temporary loophole. It is, in fact, in SAS's interest that deregulation legislation be put through as quickly as possible so as to take advantage of lucrative central European markets as well as to force the low-cost issue. Until that happens, though, Carlzon and his team are adopting a philosophy best summarised in the following words:

> Flexibility is becoming imperative and that is tough, for people want stability and long-term solutions . . . [This is only one example of] how difficult it is to change a corporate culture that is based on stability in the marketplace to one based on flexibility in a competitive environment. It's a question of culture and tradition in a context where people have been used to thinking they know what the future will bring. We propose a culture that promotes flexibility, that is receptive to change, accepting the fact that we know nothing about the future. (Jan Carlzon to the **American Management Association 20 April 1988**)

Part III
European Consumer Goods

9   Belfe Clothes:[1] 'L'Eleganza nello Sport'

The European clothing industry comprises over 28 000 firms, 75 per cent of which employ fewer than a hundred people. Though not directly affected by the prospect of European unification scheduled for the end of 1992, it is a sector that stands to witness a great deal of internal upheaval, in the form of restructuring, as it struggles to remain competitive in an environment that is rapidly taking on the aspect of a global market. The restructuring is already visible as many medium-sized companies have gone out of business or merged or fallen prey to absorption by large multinationals, such as in the case of Dim, recently bought by the American company, Sara Lee.

The largest challenges ahead are perhaps those being faced by the medium-sized companies, which, despite significant investment in manpower, image and technology, often lack the resources as well as the critical mass needed to achieve the widespread economies of scale so eagerly sought by the multinationals. A glimpse at a successful clothing firm, located near Vicenza at the foot of the Dolomite mountains in northern Italy, can help us to understand the factors upon which hinge the future success of such medium-sized firms.

AN HISTORICAL OVERVIEW

The year 1920 saw the creation of Belloni e Festa S.A. (to become known as Belfe), a company founded with the intention of making

---

1. In addition to information obtained during the course of interviews at Belfe, further data was supplied in the form of a study conducted by Chiara Cecchinato and Luigi Purgato of the Consorzio Universitario per gli Studi di Organizzazione Aziendale. This study was made available by Belfe.

and selling woven goods and waterproofed garments destined to be used as sportswear and informal, leisure time clothing. The founders of Belfe were already ahead of their time in that they quickly instilled a corporate mission, aimed at making their firm synonymous with quality, style and service. They wanted to ensure that their future clients would be guaranteed an optimal price–quality relationship with a wide variety of choice in products.

Business went well and, in the 1930s, Belfe introduced the now-classic leather jacket for motorcyclists, thus gaining a reputation for being innovative and competent in the making of complex clothing. The Second World War heralded bad times for a majority of companies around the world, yet Belfe managed to make the best of a bad situation, turning the war to its advantage with the production of windjackets and army tents, hence reinforcing its reputation as a maker of top-quality clothes and outdoor accessories. Subsequently, capitalising on experience accumulated during the war years, the windjacket was introduced commercially in two colours (navy and burgundy) in 1948, to great acclaim.

In 1951, hoping to take advantage of post-war growth, a sincere effort was made to create a wider brand awareness: it was at this time that Belfe introduced the slogan 'l'eleganza nello sport', a slogan which is still known today and symbolises the style and quality of Belfe's clothes, regardless of their designated use.

The period between 1951 and 1976 saw Belfe grow steadily, though perhaps in a haphazard way, as is so often characteristic of family-run companies. The company created a name for itself in the Italian market, but, internally, it lacked the necessary professionalism to see it securely through the approaching decade. In 1976, Angelo Carlo Festa succeeded his father as President of Belfe. Determined to transform the family company into a professional, internationally competitive firm, Festa began a process of reorganisation aimed at taking advantage of a prospering world economy and a growing consumer interest in sports and sportswear.

BELFE TODAY

In 1990, Belfe had a total sales level of 112 billion lire, divided in the following manner:

Active sports:	56 billion
Sportswear:	44.5 billion
Leather:	11.5 billion

This represented a 24 per cent increase over the previous year's sales (see Table 9.1) and reflected the progress being made due to the streamlining of operations and a progressively larger coverage of the market.

Part of the streamlining of Belfe has involved an overall restructuring of the corporate organisation chart (see Figures 9.1 and 9.2) along divisional lines in an effort to gain proximity to the various target markets. There are three major product divisions (active sports, sportswear and leather) which share the administrative, commercial/marketing and production functions; of these, only the leather goods division has a separate production line. As part of the new corporate philosophy being adopted, the senior management would like to see a great deal of divisional autonomy and thus allows divisional managers to implement the indicated strategies as they think best; they are ultimately judged on quantitative results.

Once the guiding strategies are handed down to the respective divisions, the managers are responsible for maximising profits and sales volume, while ensuring that their real costs are minimised, or at least with little or no variance from the standard costs. Though the structure appears rigid on paper, a point is made of creating an

Table 9.1 Belfe SpA: sales 1980–90 (in billions of lire)

	Sales
1980	23
1981	25
1982	27.6
1983	32.1
1984	41
1985	56
1986	68.7
1987	78.5
1988	83.3
1989	90
1990	112

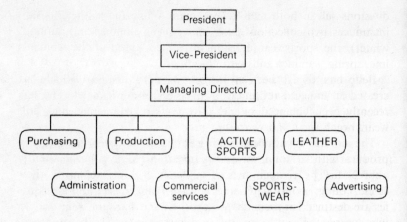

Figure 9.1 Belfe SpA: organisation chart

Figure 9.2 Belfe SpA: divisional organisation chart

informal atmosphere with easy cross communication: only the leather goods division remains slightly outside in that, in 1990, it was transformed into an independent company. This division, with sales of approximately 11 billion lire in 1990, requires different production processes as well as a different commercial structure and thus it was felt that its needs could best be met on an independent basis. This division consists of two brands: Postcard and Belfe.

The Products

Belfe makes all kinds of informal clothes and accessories (with the exception of shoes and underwear) related to sports and leisure. All divisions sell to both men and women. While the leather division introduces two collections each year (spring/summer and autumn/ winter), the sportswear division introduces three in the women's line: spring, summer and autumn/winter.

Belfe has always been strong in ski clothes, a fact which has created an unnecessary amount of seasonality in its sales. This has recently been balanced by the introduction of a tennis line, golf wear, beach wear and warm-up suits.

The aim has always been, and remains, to produce a high-quality product with a 'total' or co-ordinated look, a concept usually appreciated by retailers who find it helpful in increasing their sales. Young, sophisticated and unique, Belfe clothes and accessories are destined for men and women between the ages of 25 and 45 who enjoy the outdoors and socialising, are health-conscious, ecologically minded and have an increasing amount of free time. They are individuals who are active, feel good about themselves and want to maintain a certain fashionable look.

Production

Production design at Belfe remains complicated and is directed by the division managers, an internal stylist and a 'time and motion' team. Together, they oversee the process in its entirety, from the creative design to the final production. Along each step of the way, studies are carried out to determine whether or not the production process adopted falls into the specified cost limitations as determined by the desired price and the chosen market segment; should the parameters be exceeded, either the fabric or the design are altered, or possibly the sourcing. At the present time, part of the production is in-house and part is subcontracted.

Always conscious of marketing a unique product, great care is taken to create, each season, a range of 'Belfe' colours and so all fabrics and colours supplied are exclusive to Belfe.

Distribution

Belfe sells to over 4000 retail outlets around the world, 2000 of which are in Italy. The retail outlets chosen are usually specialists in sportswear and sports articles and reflect the desired upmarket image of Belfe products.

As a result of Belfe's personalised approach to the retail trade, it has managed to create a great deal of brand loyalty. Part of the personalised approach has included such efforts as providing money-back guarantees during the winter ski season,[2] a sales tactic which has proved to be very successful to date. The money-back guarantee was created as a way to stimulate sales during three successive poor winters and was done in collaboration with Lloyds of London. With the doubling of insurance premiums, however, this action was stopped in 1990.

Internally, Belfe's respective divisional managers are responsible for sales in the United States, Canada, Japan, Australia, South Korea and Hong Kong, while a special export manager oversees all sales within Europe and Turkey. In Italy, there are twenty-eight exclusive agents, while, abroad, there are sixteen exclusive agents and eight importers.

Advertising and Promotion

Belfe has spent seventy years creating a solid world brand. Registered in 1920, the initial logo reflected the informal aspect of Belfe products. In 1970, the original logo was changed to a more stylised form, to portray not only the informality of the products, but also the more technical or sporty side as well.

Advertising and promotion are regarded as an integral part of Belfe's strategy and as a result the company works in very close association with its agency, which is charged with the task of translating Belfe's desired image into the appropriate creative form and then choosing the best media available.

Of a total 1990 budget of approximately 6.2 billion lire (see Table 9.2), 3.9 billion were destined for advertising and the remainder for promotional campaigns, such as shopping bags, point of sale material and special sponsorship programmes. Belfe recently sponsored a Formula 1 race in collaboration with the multinational ICI, of which Belfe is a client.

---

2. Should there be a lack of natural snow by a certain agreed date, usually just before Christmas, the retailer is reimbursed for excess stock of up to a maximum value of 30 million lire. The stock, however, remains the property of the retailer.

Table 9.2 Belfe SpA: a breakdown of advertising expenditure (in millions of lire)

	Active sports	Sportswear/leather	Total
Television	1 880	–	1 880
Press	890	1 130	890
Total	2 770	1 130	3 900
Worldwide expenditure:			
Italy	4 900		
Other	1 300		
Total	6 200		

FACING THE 1990s

The 1980s saw an increase in the volume of clothing and accessories imported from non-EC countries, primarily from the Far East. These imports are expected to increase over the years to come, as European import quotas are slowly relaxed. This, together with an increase in European productivity, resulted in an overall decrease in employment in the clothing and textiles industries, aggravated yet further by unfavourable demographic trends, in the form of ageing and stagnant or decreasing populations.

Fearing the potential consequences of such trends, the industry began to undergo a certain amount of restructuring, which is expected to continue into the 1990s. On the one hand, the down-stream elements of the industry are becoming more fragmented, while upstream distributors are concentrating themselves in the hope of being able to gain broader market coverage, thus increasing economies of scale and reducing overheads (for example, advertising costs). Medium-sized companies, on the other hand, are struggling to rationalise as they scramble to secure a national or a European position through one of two alternative strategies: mass volume and hence possible large economies of scale, or focusing on niches. So far, many of these medium-sized companies appear to have chosen the latter, and, more specifically, the higher-end luxury goods market, which avoids direct competition with Asian manufacturers and allows for significantly higher margins.

In Europe as a whole, the ominous arrival of 1992 holds little in store for the clothing industry directly. However, manufacturers will gradually be able to consolidate their international strategies as price differences become less marked and as the service industries become pan-European. With ease of transport, insurance and banking expected to increase in the years to come, companies conducting business across European borders can only benefit, as they take advantage of lower costs and improved service. This will be most likely to result in further investment outside companies' domestic markets.

From the retailers' perspective, suppliers who will have the most success in the future are those that can meet the following criteria (in order of decreasing importance, as identified during a survey carried out in Italy in 1990):

● fashion and style/high brand awareness
● reliable quality (fabric and finish)
● professionalism in conducting business
● a well-adapted product line (not necessarily too large)
● ease of payment
● price stability
● product innovation
● strong advertising and promotional support
● sales assistance and advice.

Belfe, in examining itself with respect to the above criteria and to the evolution of their industry and markets as a whole, has found itself to be in a relatively good position when compared to leading competitors. However, there are certain areas that need perfecting.

While, on the one hand, the existing clients are extremely happy with the products and the personalised service, they remain somewhat unsatisfied with the delivery lead times which, in the industry as a whole, can be from six to nine months – Belfe has succeeded in greatly reducing this factor by making to order. Furthermore, though Belfe products are known for style and quality, factors widely regarded as Belfe's competitive advantage in the sportswear markets, it is felt by many that the existing product line is too large and needs to be reduced, to facilitate buying and inventories.

Internally, Belfe finds itself in a particularly solid financial situation, thus allowing for the auto-financing of ambitious modernisation projects. In an effort to decrease costs, Belfe is concentrating on two areas: decreasing stock levels and increasing labour productivity through investment in highly mechanised fabric cutting machines and mechanised warehouse facilities. The Belfe management believes, as do many, that the future success of a company could hinge quite simply on the incorporation of modern, high-technology methods into production and design (that is, CAD–CAM).

The leather division differentiates itself slightly from the active sports and sportswear divisions in that the strategy presently being opted for is that of reaching and exceeding what is deemed to be the critical volume production level. With annual sales of 11 billion lire, Belfe would like to see the division reach 30 billion lire. To do so, the division not only makes its own-label clothes, but also those of other well-known clothes designers, such as Giorgio Armani.

On the competitive front, as mentioned, the Far East manufacturers are a threat. However, closer to home, Italy boasts over 350 clothing manufacturers, 200 of whom manufacture under their own labels. Despite this proliferation of local companies, Belfe has thus far held its own and even managed to increase its market share.

'Made in Italy', however, is no longer enough to guarantee success. Belfe aims to be a leader in sportswear and accessories, yet remains with a fairly low brand awareness outside the home market. In an attempt to correct this, efforts in the near future will be aimed at creating a strong international brand through the use of extensive advertising and promotion. As part of this strategy, Belfe has recently begun a process of significant investment in Japan and South Korea as well as the United States, where it is represented by a commercial agent. In Japan, the mode of entry chosen has been through a joint venture with Seibu, a leading Japanese department store chain employing over 30 000 people. Thus far, Belfe has forty-one points of sale in that market. In South Korea, on the other hand, Belfe has opted to enter the market via an import agent who presently has fourteen points of sale. Once firmly established in these markets, Belfe would like to expand throughout South-East Asia.

The key will be not only to create a strong international image, but to reinforce that image with continued quality, style and innovation as well as superior service.

10 The Mexx Group: Textbook Innovation at Work

The Corporate Design headquarters of the Mexx Group, situated in a quiet suburb of The Hague, recently won a prize as one of the seven most innovative buildings in the world. From the outside, it is an attractive nineteenth-century grey and white building set in wooded grounds; on the inside, it is a spacious, post-modernist structure in which a visitor is immediately struck by its luxury. It is an office complex more in line with what one would expect from a prestigious advertising agency rather than a clothes designer/wholesaler. Yet, this building, in combining a sense of order and structure together with creativity, succeeds in symbolising not only the success of the Mexx Group, but also its management philosophy. Though not without its share of problems, the Mexx Group is, by most standards, a success story.

THE ORIGINS

The Mexx Group was created in the early 1980s by two men from India who came to The Netherlands in search of new opportunities, though without a clear objective. It was when one of the founders became interested in fashion and clothes, by way of his girlfriend, that the idea of creating a truly different line of clothing came to mind.

Rattan Chadha arrived in The Netherlands from his native India in 1970, after having obtained an MBA. Together with his colleague P. K. Sen Sharma, they felt that opportunities existed in Europe if they could take advantage of India's low manufacturing costs and act as importers of 'prêt-à-porter' clothes. In parallel with the newly-created import agency, a chain of small retail outlets, known as 'Didi', was set up. This second business experienced rapid growth during the 1970s, but was to be hard hit by the economic slump of

1978. Finding themselves with a warehouse full of unwanted stock, both businesses were sold in 1979.

It was then that Chadha and Sharma came up with a new idea for a line of clothing. The initial concept was to put on the market a line of co-ordinated casual clothes for men and women. Operating on a basis of subcontracting, primarily to manufacturers in the Far East, the Emanuelle and Moustache lines quickly gained popularity in Europe as well as North America, selling through chain stores.

However, as the popularity of the two lines increased in the mid-1980s the founders began to encounter trademark problems. The net result of these problems were a lack of consistency and logic in the product lines' image across borders (for example, while Moustache would be the men's line in one country, legal problems forced it to become a women's line in another). It became clear that a new identity would need to be created to consolidate the image of the group. The initial idea was 'ME'; however, this was blocked by Brooke Shields, the actress, who already held a trademark of the same name. Finally, the founders stumbled upon 'Mexx' (M for Moustache, E for Emanuelle and two Xs for kisses) and it stuck.

The transition from Emanuelle and Moustache to Mexx occurred during a six-month period in 1986, when all three lines were introduced simultaneously. The transition phase was also taken advantage of to reposition Mexx more as a lifestyle than an article of clothing, aimed to appeal to a slightly higher segment than the original Emanuelle and Moustache lines, a strategy which initially caused some customer confusion: while Emanuelle and Moustache were firmly perceived as volume products in many markets, Mexx was now trying to compete on a different and higher quality level. This was further aggravated by the lack of involvement of country subsidiaries in the transition period as well as the overall economic situation: 'Unfortunately, Mexx found itself implementing its repositioning policy at a difficult time in the company's existence. It was confronted with a stagnating market, with fierce price competition from numerous fashion companies and insufficient brand awareness to go with that'.[1]

---

1. The Nijenrode School of Business case entitled 'The Mexx Group – Part B', by Rose Marie Boudeguer and Gerard B. J. Bomers, 1991.

The Mexx Management then embarked on a series of strategy changes in an attempt to re-educate the customers and find a firm niche within the marketplace: 'We kept changing . . . We travelled all over the marketplace. We went from casual volume marketing to casual premium marketing . . . We lost our identity and confused customers and final consumers alike'.[2]

THE TURNING POINT

The turning point in Mexx's first decade of operations came in 1987. Based on the premise that the company's ultimate success was dependent on having close contacts with the final consumer, the directors began to feel competitive pressure to invest in retail outlets, to secure both margins and control over distribution. However, such a strategic move would require a great deal of capital, which the directors were thinking of obtaining by going public. Not willing to embark upon such a venture without an outside opinion, a consulting team was called in to evaluate the prospects and opportunities. What the team discovered was a creative organisation that had experienced growth without a solid guiding hand. While it was clear that Mexx had a product that worked, it did not have the managerial support needed to ensure a profitable future. In essence, Mexx lacked direction and structure, as identified by two of the company's senior managers: 'Mexx lacks sufficient systems to support a retail strategy . . . We are neither manufacturers nor retailers, we are a wholesale company'.[3]

The plans for going public and for investing in retail were abandoned and a process of rapid and drastic reorganisation began, under the guidance of a senior manager recruited from the consulting team. The premise of the reorganisation was 'to start from zero'; It was as if Mexx was beginning anew. In an astonishing four months, Mexx was reborn, having gone through a process of creating new positions, defining job profiles and hiring individuals – the entire structure that exists today is skill-based. In concrete terms, the positions created were defined from the top down and

2. Ibid.
3. Ibid.

each time a new person came in, they collaborated in defining the job profiles for the positions to follow below. However, throughout this process, salesmen were never 'let go'.

Once in place, the new management then embarked upon the arduous task of identifying a strategy for the future. At the root of the strategy ultimately adopted lies the corporate philosophy that the Mexx directors have succeeded in creating.

CREATING A CORPORATE PHILOSOPHY

The Mexx Group is comprised of approximately 1000 people worldwide, representing almost every corner of the Earth. Of these 1000, thirty-five are designers exclusive to the group and sixteen come under the wing of the strategic marketing department which is, in turn, organised by product line.

While most design companies around the world can be described as being guided by 'feeling', the Mexx management prides itself on having created a market-driven company whose structure is based on the model American consumer-goods company. The Mexx management views design as a business and succeeds in running it as such. This is perhaps best symbolised by the layout of its headquarters, which is in two buildings: in one are the sales, distribution and financial services, and in the other, the design and marketing functions. The link between marketing and design, so often ignored, is regarded as essential to the success of the group; each side must be in constant contact with the other in order to understand what the market wants and what the limitations of the company are. The designers are there to be creative, but that creativity must fall within acceptable limits, as defined by the market and communicated by the marketers.

At the heart of Mexx's strategy lies the 'concept cycle', developed by Rattan Chadha. The 'concept cycle' aims to create a co-ordinated system 'whereby the different disciplines of the company's operational structure are intertwined in a continuous and self-perpetuating cycle. The underlying philosophy is that all elements of the Group must operate like a clock . . .'.[4]

---

4. Ibid.

The Corporate Philosophy

Part of the 'concept cycle's' objective is to create a single corporate philosophy which will help all the employees to work towards the most efficient system possible. The creation of this corporate identity is embodied in the 'Concept Manual', distributed to all employees, whether designers, salesmen or marketing directors.

The 'Concept Manual'

A quick look at the contents of the manual helps to convey the underlying links between the various departments of Mexx as perceived by the company's founders:

A.　Consumer ideal and target
B.　Products – philosophy
C.　Designing – philosophy
D.　Marketing
　　　– philosophy
　　　– competitive status
　　　– ideal retailer
　　　– wholesale strategy
E.　Merchandising
F.　Sales policies
G.　Samples
H.　Pricing
I.　Production
J.　Shipping
K.　Promotion
L.　Corporate strategy
M.　Group image/identity
N.　Manual definitions.

This manual, because of its scope, is regarded as indispensable in the conduct of daily business.

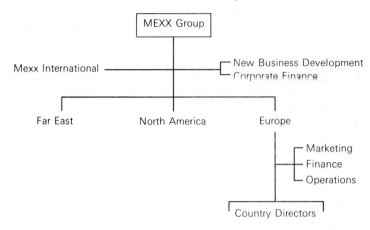

Figure 10.1   The Mexx Group: internal organisation

However, the running of a business does not stop at the link between marketing and design. To allow for centralised control that nevertheless incorporates a certain degree of managerial freedom, the Mexx management has put in place a complicated internal structure based on a matrix system (see Figure 10.1). Along one side of the matrix are the marketing, finance and operations directors, along the other are the country managers. While the country managers are ultimately responsible for their financial performance, it is the functional directors who manage the product lines across borders and who are judged on their overall performance. At the top of the matrix is the director of Mexx Europe (or Far East or North America) whose job it is to communicate the corporate strategy and convince the managers of its validity, the objective being to work on a consensus basis. However, despite this consensus approach, it is the Mexx divisional director who has the final word.

This combination of creativity with a certain managerial rigidity extends well beyond the concept of corporate structure, into every aspect of the overall business.

PRODUCTION AND OPERATIONS

The scope of business presently managed by the Mexx Group requires well-thought-out logistics with a great deal of planning.

The original concept of sub-contracting all production has been maintained, as has the policy of zero stock. While the former implies a certain flexibility as well as a significantly lower capital investment and risk level, the latter counters this by instilling a rigidity with clients which is out of the ordinary in this industry. In order to maintain a zero stock level, all products in the making are pre-sold. Should clients arrive one day too late, they are turned away. This policy is, in fact, what allowed Mexx to get started in the first place, despite a lack of financial resources, as pre-selling significantly diminishes any financial risk.

On the other hand, should a client place an order in time, he will be pleasantly surprised with the method of delivery of the final product. While most clothing designers and wholesalers have a policy of delivering an entire collection at once (though usually late), Mexx has devised a mechanism whereby a season's collection is delivered in three instalments, equally divided over three months (each instalment arriving on the first day of the month). Though this policy incurs slightly higher costs for Mexx, it is received with great enthusiasm by the clients, who see their shops replenished on a regular basis and with a completely new look each time, not to mention the lower inventory costs incurred. For Mexx, it means positioning itself as a fashion leader within its chosen segment. To date, Mexx has a record of 97 per cent delivery, meaning that 97 per cent of all deliveries are correct and on time.

The Mexx design group is responsible for all fabric designs, which are created on a CAD–CAM system, and does all its own buying of fabrics. The designs are then completed in Hong Kong four times a year, Hong Kong being where 75 per cent of Mexx's subcontracted production takes place.

However, in an effort to have more product choice, part of the production presently done in Hong Kong is being centralised by being transferred to Europe, a strategy which is very different from that of Italian-based Benetton, which is adopting a policy of sourcing production close to the point of sale. While the primary reason for Mexx's move is to enlarge its product choice, it cannot be overlooked that production costs in the Far East, traditionally among the lowest in the world, are increasing as are standards of quality. Mexx views itself as having a policy of global sourcing.

The transfer of part of the production from Hong Kong to Europe (not expected to exceed 40 per cent) does bring with it certain problems. On the human side, a staff of 320 people in Hong Kong needs to be cut down and/or transferred, while, on the production side, the quantity of returns for European production have been higher than the usual 1 per cent or less experienced in the Far East. Returns in Europe are now in line with Hong Kong levels due to extensive quality control on the part of Mexx.

PRICING

The clothing industry is characterised by aggressive pricing as manufacturers aim to cover rising costs while gaining market share. Most companies have a policy of setting price according to costs and subsequent desired margins, but Mexx has ensured that its market-driven philosophy rules this most sensitive of areas.

While the concept is simple, the realisation is extremely complex. So that the marketing department can establish retail prices to suit the market, salesmen are asked to take note of competitor prices in five countries identified as primary markets. These samples are then placed in a database and analysed to give the range of possible prices which Mexx will be able to charge and which will succeed in positioning the products in the desired segment. After deducting the desired margins, the Mexx design team then determines which fabrics and designs can be used that stay within the identified cost structure. This in turn will determine the possible sources. This system has been in place for approximately a year and now needs a complete overhaul of the existing information system to provide a sophisticated database. Ideally, Mexx would like to see, in the future, the creation of a computerised distribution and market research system such as 'levi-link' which is directly connected to the retail outlets, thereby providing sales data in real time.

NEW PRODUCT DEVELOPMENT

New product development, often seen as the most creative aspect of this sector, remains so at Mexx, though within a predetermined time frame and structure that could seem stifling to other clothing designers. Rather than launch a new line of clothes and hope that it will prove to be a success, the Mexx marketing and design team plan up to one and a half years ahead. Based on research, a product line is developed in the form of a pilot collection which is subsequently tested with the desired retailers and consumers through the use of interviews, focus groups and questionnaires. In this way, products which do not meet the buying criteria of the consumer can be altered or redesigned, so allowing expensive mistakes to be avoided.

MEXX'S TARGET MARKET

Mexx presently looks to men and women between the ages of 20 and 35 as their principal markets. In addition, a 'teens and kids' line has been introduced, aimed at girls and boys between the ages of three and fifteen (kids: 3–7, teens: 8–15); a 'mini' line is expected in 1992 for the 0–2-year -old group. Of total sales, estimated at 275 million dollars, 25 per cent are from the men's line, 40 per cent from the women's line and the remaining 35 per cent from the teens and kids lines.

MEXX'S IMAGE IN THE MARKET: KEEPING UP WITH THE TIMES

Initially, the Emanuelle and Moustache lines were positioned more as a lifestyle rather than a product, cultivating a somewhat unconventional or even wild state of mind. This trend continued and is still evident today in the Mexx catalogues, as shown by the fabric and clothes designs.

However, a change in consumer mentality together with a change in corporate philosophy has resulted in a slightly altered positioning to keep pace with the times. The more rebellious outlooks of the 1970s and early 1980s have given way to the return of traditional values all while maintaining and stressing individual differences. Perhaps the mindset of the 1990s is best embodied in the statements printed throughout the Mexx catalogues:

'Beginning meaningful relationships with our affirmation of a green world, a community of friends, the love of diversity, traditional quality and new values.'

'honest, simple, and real . . . a mood a caring, an environment of people who share'

'every canvas begins with colour, the Mexx palette for the artist is you . . .'

'discovering a new spirit, sharing an optimistic outlook, embracing unlimited possibilities'

The Mexx image of the 1990s puts forth a spirit of internationalism and cultural diversity, in many respects similar to that presented by Benetton. Yet, unlike Benetton, where the entire emphasis is on their multicultural theme, Mexx would like to place more importance on the product itself. Whereas in Benetton ads one sees pictures of people from around the world, but with Benetton products hardly ever in view, Mexx ensures that its products are easily identifiable within the setting chosen to symbolise the new values.

Mexx management would like to think of their product as being 'modern' and in step with the evolution of its target segment. This provides a formidable challenge for the marketing and design teams in that they must have the foresight to predict what will be popular with at least 18 months lead time to the introduction of a new collection, as dictated by the internal planning schedules.

LOOKING TO THE FUTURE: KEEPING AHEAD IN THE 1990s

The fall of the Berlin Wall appeared as an omen for the decade that was beginning. Not only did it bring about displays of solidarity around the world, with parades, concerts, speeches and political statements designed officially to usher in a new age, but it seemed to wake managers up to the fact that indeed times were changing and it could prove to be an opportune moment to revise corporate strategies if they were to keep pace with events.

In reality, the effects of the opening up of Eastern Europe will be slow in coming. Instead, the real opportunities that are presenting themselves are those that have been in the making for the last twenty years: European economic unification, growing environmentalism, changing technologies, the rise of South-east Asia as an economic force and the globalisation of markets, to mention only a few. It is these all-important developments, so often overlooked in the past by managers concerned with their companies' day-to-day operations, that the Mexx management began to address between 1987 and 1990.

As previously mentioned, the short-term concerns revolved around creating a more professional staff capable of overseeing the complicated operations of the Mexx Group as well as planning ahead. During the process of reorganisation and planning, with most of the attention shifted inward, sales slipped somewhat. This was nevertheless taken advantage of in that it allowed Mexx to further consolidate its image by eliminating those clients that no longer fitted the emerging corporate philosophy.

The consolidation of Mexx's image fell within the new guidelines of the orchestrated marketing plan being put into place. The next stage was to identify the opportunities that lay ahead.

Looking initially at Mexx's position in their leading markets, it became clear that substantial room for growth existed. While France and Germany are the countries contributing most to sales and profits, the brand awareness has been estimated at only 8 per cent and 11 per cent respectively. It would appear that a significant increase in these levels of brand awareness could lead to corresponding increases in sales. But how to do this with the limited resources available? While local and regional differences are important, financial resources and corporate identity strategies dictate a certain degree of image streamlining; the cost of developing campaigns can be prohibitive, particularly if each market insists on its own communications plan. The liberalisation of advertising and media legislation in Europe, together with a consumer profile which is ever more transferable across borders are making such a challenge manageable. On the one hand, satellite television is becoming commonplace throughout Europe and the world (one need only look at the global success of the US-based CNN–Cable News Network during the Gulf Crisis or at the availability of SkyChannel and Super Channel in Europe) and, on the other hand, younger consumers are increasingly 'similar in their difference', due in large part to the proliferation of the media; individuality is essential, but the themes are global, as witnessed so well in the fall of the Berlin Wall. This unusual combination of circumstances allows for the creation of global campaigns which appeal to the consumers' sense of values and well-being, themes particularly suited to Mexx's products. At the base of this lies the Mexx management's premise that the modern-day individual is conscious of the events that are occurring around him

In addition to gaining market share in Europe,[5] Mexx is currently planning additional expansion in Japan and Korea through an agreement with a leading trading company. This expansion is expected to take place during the next two years.

Having taken advantage of opportunities provided on the outside, the Mexx management has been able turn inwards to try to capitalise even further on the macro-trends taking place. Of key importance are the potential economies of scale related to media-buying. While such financial gains are still disputed, it seems clear that companies can obtain some profit from the centralised buying of space as well as from the availability of pan-European media. But financial and organisational gains from economies of scale go beyond media buying to include marketing planning, financial planning and staffing.

A global approach has given way to a reduced, centralised Mexx marketing staff responsible for the implementation of a world strategy co-ordinated on a consensus basis, as discussed previously, with the various country managers. Mexx now introduces global collections as opposed to national collections, so cutting down on planning times, necessary personnel and complex logistics.

Operating across geographic borders implies an uncomfortable reliance on the proper functioning of the exchange-rate mechanism. Should there be a sudden and unexpected fluctuation in exchange rates, financial results at year end can, as a result, be either much

---

5. Increasing market share within Europe can be a difficult proposition due to quota restrictions imposed by governments for products being sourced out of non-EC countries. While these quotas are gradually being eased, they remain extremely difficult to obtain. The quotas are established according to company and to item and are sold on an auction basis. These quotas have, for instance, made it almost impossible for Mexx to gain entry into the Spanish market. Furthermore, one of Mexx's key success factors is the concept of co-ordinated clothing. As quotas are by item, importing co-ordinated lines can be next to impossible.

higher or much lower than expected. The Mexx directors feel that savings can be obtained from their centralised structure due in large part to the multicultural aspect of its staff. The financial staff is knowlcdgcablc on currency transactions and capital markets around the world and is capable of working across borders with ease; currency hedging is handled efficiently with a limited staff.

Such opportunities as mentioned above are available to virtually any company operating across borders. The key is in the implementation of the chosen strategies. In this respect, Mexx regards the future as hingeing not on the choice of a global, multiregional or local strategy, but on making the necessary investments in information technology and management skills.

In order to be able to run and control a market-driven business, it is necessary to understand the market and to have the necessary information. The key is information; the information needed to make astute operations and strategy decisions must be correctly identified and must be processed in the most efficient manner possible. This requires considerable investment in computer technology as well as in human resources.

The Mexx manager of the future will be a generalist who sees things in black and white. To those working for him he will give the tools necessary to get the job done, but he will not wait; if a task is not done in the allotted time, the manager must be able and willing to step in and do it himself. In essence, Mexx would like to instil an American management philosophy into the lines of the structure it has adopted.

Mexx has known ten years of success, albeit with a few ups and downs, and it is intent on experiencing another decade of yet more success, though not necessarily growth. At the beginning, the secret lay in an innovative product that worked. It was the right product at the right time. Today, the gamble for the future is on adopting a pan-European and global approach within an organisational concept that follows, almost to the letter, a marketing textbook, updated with sophisticated control measures based on an equally sophisticated information system. Whether or not the present strategy, based on an innovative and difficult combination of creativity and organisational control, will succeed, remains unknown; what is certain is that, in an increasingly difficult economic and market environment, the medium-sized Mexx will give the larger competitors a run for their money.

11 Amorim Lage, S.A.: Pasta from Portugal?

This book so far has presented to the reader a cross-section of European companies and has attempted to give an insight into the particular problems and opportunities that lie ahead for each one as their managers prepare not only for a new decade but for a new century. The majority if not all of the company managers interviewed have a plan, or the semblance of one, to guarantee their respective company's survival and prosperity. While unforeseen events such as the 1991 Gulf War may destabilise the natural course of events in the short term, it would seem a fair statement to say that, in the long run, opportunities abound: trade barriers within Europe are falling, Eastern Europe is slowly opening up, consumers are becoming more homogeneous, distribution chains are simplifying, and so on – these trends and opportunities can all be profitably taken advantage of by those who have the vision to see them, the daring to take them and the wherewithal to ensure their own survival. Yet it must be remembered by executives and politicians alike that economies are not made up only of multinationals with extensive financial and human resources at their disposal, but rather of small and medium-sized companies, often family-run, whose managers are caught up in day-to-day affairs and who do not have a staff of analysts whose function it is to obtain a full understanding of the significance and the impact of macro-political and economic events in the stratospheres above them. While the multinationals may go on existing, whether governments rise or fall, the small and medium-sized enterprises may not. If they do not, Europe will lose what can be considered the backbone of many of its countries' economies and social structures.

Portugal, situated on the westernmost reaches of the European continent, is perhaps the best example of an economy based on small and medium-sized companies: only 1.5 per cent of the total companies registered actually qualify as being large enterprises, according to European Community standards. Amorim Lage, S.A., situated in Oporto, offers an example of the type of situation being confronted by many managers of small and medium-sized businesses as well as of the many business and economic disparities that still exist between the various member countries of the European Community.

Unlike the cases presented in earlier chapters, with Amorim Lage the senior managers face a situation in which they are obliged to sail uncharted waters; the highly-regulated market situation that existed in Portugal until the late 1970s has gradually given way to the now open competitive environment. They are aware, as are their competitors, of the threats and opportunities that loom ahead. Yet it can be difficult to reconcile half a decade of recent history with almost seventy years of family management style.

Amorim Lage's (AL) main business is, on the one hand, the production and sale of dried pasta and, on the other, the production of flour for industrial use. Making up only 5 per cent of the total sales is the production and sale of biscuits and cakes for retail sale (see Table 11.1).

Table 11.1   Development of Amorim Lage's sales, 1984–89 (in millions of escudos)

	Pasta	Flour	Biscuits and cakes	Other
1984	1049	1022	93	39
1985	1399	1286	136	56
1986	1538	1418	165	67
1987	1545	1580	189	75
1988	1609	1732	200	94
1989	1701	1630	222	105

While the focus of this case-study will be on the pasta division, it is nevertheless interesting to have an understanding of the industrial flour market. In the 1950s, the majority of bakeries were small, family-run outlets. AL, realising that gains could be made by integrating vertically, became the first food company to attempt to do so by making bread for the retail market and selling it through its wholly-owned retail network. In many respects, AL's management had a good idea at the wrong time – it was too early. This became particularly evident when the government, considering bread as an essential item of merchandise, began taking an active interest in bread distribution and eventually put into place strict price controls. The net result of this, combined with increasing costs, was the inability of manufacturers such as AL to stay afloat financially. By the 1970s, most of the original manufacturers had divested themselves of bread distribution points and concentrated upstream in the supply of raw material, that is, flour, and AL proved to be no exception.

Today, this situation prevails, though the financial ailments of the original actors have not disappeared. Downstream, the industry is characterised by an extremely fragmented market, while upstream and situated in the North of Portugal there are essentially seven producers of industrial flour; these are regarded as the main competitors as, thus far, the producers based in the Centre and South have not made their presence felt. While it would seem that the raw-material suppliers, because of their relative size, could control the market price, they are faced with a standard product whose success depends only on price. Rather than co-operate with one another, the flour producers have engaged in price wars and have initiated a process of acquisitions, both friendly and hostile. This trend of mergers and acquisitions has now given way to the creation of two groups, one of which (Harmonia) AL effectively controls. In addition, AL also controls 50 per cent of a company situated in the centre of Portugal.

The future, viewed from the present time, is apt to be seen in terms of market stagnation, despite a slight trend towards the increasing popularity of speciality breads and biscuits.

The production of dried pasta brings to the forefront an altogether different situation, requiring a more global perspective in order to understand the competitive processes at work both within and outside Portugal.

In Southern Europe, pasta has gained rapid popularity due to its good price–quality relationship. Elsewhere, the increase in international travel combined with the proliferation of ethnic restaurants the world over has resulted in the ever-rising popularity of new foods. People are more curious and more willing to experiment with the unknown, or simply to try something old in a new form. For instance, today, even if one is hopelessly lost in the cluttered cross-streets of Taipei, in Taiwan, one can stumble upon an Italian restaurant. While the quality and the atmosphere may not remind

Table 11.2   Growth sectors in key pasta markets, 1983–87, percentage value change

Type of pasta	France	UK	US
Egg	+ 32	–	–
Egg-free	+ 28.5	–	–
Dry	–	+ 25.6	+ 30.8
Packaged dinner	–	–	+ 40.3
Canned	–	+ 7	+ 13.6
Frozen	–	+ 690.6	+ 191
Fresh	–	+ 581.8	–

Source: Euromonitor Market Direction.

you of Rome, the fact is that great cultural bridges, hitherto unimaginable, are being formed. This is equally true in Portugal.

Adding to the syndrome of 'the citizen of the world' is the growing concern of the average consumer with health and fitness. A trend originally begun in the United States during the 1970s, where it even reached advanced stages of frenzied mania, it has now spread to Northern Europe, from whence it is rapidly making its way south, as consumers discover the new potential of pasta. Concerned with avoiding preservatives and, often, meat of any kind as well as obtaining the right levels of vitamins, these health-conscious invidivuals have sought new foods to vary what could otherwise be considered by some to be a bland diet.

These general trends have together succeeded in popularising dried and fresh pasta, among other foods, and have caused the world's leading food manufacturers to get on the bandwagon, lest they be left behind, unable to capitalise on a potential boom market. Once perceived as a fattening, non-nourishing food, pasta is now welcomed as an essential element of a balanced diet. It is now recognised that pasta has nutritional value and it has the advantage of being extremely versatile.

As witness to this race for a share of the market, Nestlé recently acquired the Italian company Buitoni; French BSN has acquired another of Italy's leading producers; and such conglomerates as Heinz, Borden, Philip-Morris/General Foods-Kraft and Campbell's have all begun to diversify into various types of pasta.

Yet, while pasta consumption is still experiencing modest growth, there are certain warning signs that the acquisition of market share may not be taken for granted. Italy remains the world's leading dried pasta producer but the manufacturers are faced with a significant overcapacity, due in part to a decrease in Italian pasta consumption as well as to a desire on the part of the major brand names to capitalise on the prestige of Italian food products in the export market. With Italy regarded as the home of pasta, multi-nationals such as Barilla and Buitoni have little difficulty in gaining shelf space among the leading food retailers throughout the world and they are even able to charge a premium price simply because of their origin.

The effect of Italy's overcapacity is already visible in such countries as France and Germany, where Italian imports have increased at the expense of domestic production. Second to Italy in production is the United States, where the multinationals in all sectors, from food to clothes, have begun to develop aggressive strategies for conquering the European market, before it is too late. Of note is Borden, selling in the USA, which has gained a leading position in pasta production and sales, possibly outranking in volume the leading Italian producer.

This tight global competition has resulted in a great deal of product innovation, the aim of which is to secure market share in specific niches, taking advantage of new technology such as microwave ovens, and to stay a step ahead of consumers' changing desires. One of the outcomes of this innovation has been the creation of such products as frozen pasta[1] and novelty pasta (for example, multicoloured pasta, pasta in different shapes, dessert pastas, and so on), all of which have the distinct advantage of being high-value-added products.

---

1. Pasta can be divided into two categories: that made with egg and that made with durum wheat. The former is regarded as a 'soft' pasta of lesser quality and is sold particularly in Northern Europe and the Far East. The latter, generally regarded as being of superior quality, is sold throughout Europe and North and South America. Within these two large categories, one can further subdivide into dry pasta, fresh (or chilled) pasta, frozen and canned/other.

With this brief review of the global competitive situation that exists within the pasta market, it is possible to take a closer look at Portugal and in particular at the predicament of Amorim Lage. As mentioned in Chapter 6, the 1980s witnessed the beginning of profound changes deep within the Portuguese economy. The brief Communist Government of 1974–75 succeeded, in a period of six months, in nationalising entire industries, from banking to oil to beverages. The leading Portuguese corporations rapidly became uncompetitive entities, immune from international competition, surviving in many cases on state subsidies. They quickly became overstaffed, with structures that corresponded very little with the real world either as it was then or is today. Alhough the Communists stayed in power only a short time, the damage done was extensive and it is only with the official introduction of Portugal into the European Community in 1986 that the economy has opened itself to the outside world. However, relative to the rest of Europe, the process of market liberalisation has been and continues to be a painful one for many. Aside from the differences in business practices, a weak infrastructure and the relative unsophistication of Portuguese industry, there are deeply ingrained psychological barriers (see Chapter 6) that must be overcome before Portugal can be considered an equal European partner.

With respect to the smaller companies, which make up over 95 per cent of the Portuguese economy, the period from 1975 to 1986 saw the status quo that had existed under the regimes of Salazar and Caetano maintained, as the governments were too busy restoring order and stability in the aftermath of the revolutions both at home and in the African colonies of Angola and Mozambique to make changes. The status quo simply meant that the backbone of Portugal's economy operated in a near-vacuum, totally removed from competitive processes and almost devoid of business contacts with the rest of Europe. Technology stagnated, employee productivity fell, manager motivation ebbed, marketing and finance were ignored.

As an example of how managers could slacken off, until 1974 the respective market shares of AL and its competitors were pre-determined by the government, as was the acquisition of raw material. In 1974 the situation altered in that production quotas were eliminated, but the acquisition of raw material remained under government control, being strictly monitored by a government association called EPAC (Empresa Pública da Administração de Cereais). Aimed at securing profit for the government, EPAC imported grain from the United States, but fixed the prices of cereals, such as durum wheat, the primary ingredient of pasta, at levels superior to the free market price and to European prices.

In early 1991, however, EPAC changed its legal statute to allow for the issue of shares, all of which are today held by the state. This was, in accordance with EC regulations, accompanied by an end to its monopoly. Under European Community regulations, it must now buy raw material from within the Community in order to avoid excessive taxes on imports from the United States and other non-Community countries. Furthermore, EPAC's clients now have the right to buy where they like. The net effect of this will be to lower the price of cereals, in fact, as free-market mechanisms come into place. Perhaps the key to EPAC's own survival is its effective monopoly of the grain storage facilities in Portugal, a service much sought after by its old clients.

AMORIM LAGE, S.A. – THE NEED TO BREAK FROM THE PAST

AL was founded in 1919 by Jose Alves de Amorim and Manuel Gonçalves Lage in association with a third partner, Soares, who, however, left the company in 1931 to found his own group, which subsequently failed. The initial business was that of providing flour to bakers under the brand name Paradense. The success of the venture prompted the owners to expand, building a second automated unit for the production of pasta, to be marketed under the brand name Milaneza; the two units were joined into one in 1950.

In 1958, AL began to make bread destined for direct sale to the consumer. However, production of bread remained quite limited (127 tonnes) when compared to the amount of flour produced for industrial use (1800 tonnes). The bread made was initially distributed on a door-to-door basis in the Oporto area close to the factory. Then eager to expand this activity, AL began to establish its own retail bread outlets. But despite efforts to promote its bakery division, AL felt obliged to cease this activity in 1978, when internal accounts revealed that it was only contributing to 10 per cent of total sales, while accounting for 40 per cent of total costs.

As it turns out, the sale of fresh bread is once again becoming popular, from Los Angeles to Athens. Unlike in decades past, when freshly-made bread was merely a necessity, it has today become a luxury and is sold at premium prices in specialised stores, such as the Italian chain, Il Fornaio, recently established in Portugal.

To make use of the bakery production line, once the investment had been made, AL's managers decided to enter the biscuits and cakes market. In a highly competitive environment, AL has managed to gain only 2 per cent of the Portuguese market, equivalent to 5 per cent of AL's total sales.

It is generally felt that, as the standard of living increases in Portugal and as the average consumer becomes more accustomed to shopping in large supermarkets and hypermarkets, the consumption of packaged biscuits and cookies will follow the trends seen in such countries as Italy, Spain and France, as well as Northern Europe and the UK, markets where, despite established tradition, these products have met with success. Nevertheless, because of such upswings in consumption patterns, competition is not lacking. In Portugal alone, there are seven brands distributed nationally, with the market shares shown in Table 11.3.

Table 11.3   Market shares of Portugal's leading cake
and biscuit producers, 1990 (in percentages)

Cuetara	19
Triunfo	18
Nacional	14
Pro-Alimentar	12
Vieira	8
Aliança	7
Amorim Lage	2
Other	20

With the end of protective trade barriers, success in this and other food segments will depend greatly on a company's ability to gain shelf space in the leading supermarket and hypermarket chains being set up around the country (for example, Continente and Euromarché). To do so will require a combination of low prices, good quality and prompt delivery as well as a brand name recognised by the consumer. In the case of Euromarché or Continente, a visible preference is given to known brands, often originating from the chains' home country.

Amorim Lage has a very limited brand awareness in this product category; one option is to try to expand by investing in advertising and distribution, as well as in machinery to increase capacity. Otherwise, AL could envisage continuing to supply on a local level or, ultimately, to divest themselves of this area.

Turning back to pasta, AL ranks second, with 29 per cent of the Portuguese market, behind Nacional (38 per cent) and ahead of Triunfo (15 per cent), not including the imports from Italy such as Buitoni and Barilla (see Table 11.4). Nacional, a state-owned company, is rumoured to be facing its possible demise, despite its leading market share, because of poor management at all levels. Triunfo, on the other hand, poses a credible risk to the other competitors in that it now has a competent management team whose aim is to strengthen its brand's image and distribution. With respect to geographical presence, Nacional and Triunfo are present throughout the country while AL remains unevenly spread: omnipresent in the North, its pasta is scarcer in the Centre and South, where Nacional and Triunfo dominate. Nevertheless, efforts have been made to increase market penetration in these areas, the benefits of which are beginning to be felt: AL has managed to gain a 12 per cent market share in the Lisbon area.

Table 11.4   Estimated market shares of Portuguese pasta producers, 1970–90 (in percentages)

	1970	*1990*
Nacional	16	38
Amorim Lage	6	29
Triunfo	8	15
Marco	1	11
Others	69	7

As mentioned earlier, the foreign multinationals will undoubtedly want to secure significant market shares, particularly in light of the fact that prices in Portugal are extremely low when compared to the rest of Europe (almost 50 per cent lower than retail prices in Spain) and thus, to justify their presence, they will need volume to make up for lost margin.

AL has the advantage of having a solid distribution network in the North relative to its Portuguese competitors, but it lacks the brand awareness and volume needed to be competitive with the food conglomerates. One must inevitably ask how long their distribution advantages can last.

Portugal has long since prided itself on low labour costs. With its entry into the European Community, the costs of labour are expected to increase quite rapidly until they are within an acceptable range for Europe as a whole. The effect of such a trend is already visible in industries such as textiles, where more and more family-run companies are going bankrupt or selling out to holdings. Those that will ultimately survive will be those with quality control, a product of international standing, a high level of automation and clear-cut strategies.

AL has an automated pasta factory and could benefit from the fact that making pasta is a simple process[2] as well as from its brand name Milaneza, which suggests to the consumer that the product comes from Italy. However, before doing so, certain obstacles need to be removed.

To increase AL's chances of survival, various proposals have been made ranging from a restructuring of the company based on markets and product (thus imposing a much-needed marketing philosophy to make it more flexible and more in tune with the needs of the consumer) to the introduction of high-value-added speciality pasta products, to be sold at a premium price. The latter has been approved and is scheduled to begin in 1992. Also, to further improve internal production techniques, 5 billion escudos have been invested in factory modernisation over the last few years, an investment which has been accompanied by the gradual decrease in numbers of personnel.

Having almost always operated in a controlled market, such things as advertising and promotion to the consumer are seen more as a waste of funds rather than an investment in market

---

2. The making of dried pasta consists of: cleaning the wheat, grinding, weighing, storage, mixing with water, extruding, cutting, cooking and drying, followed by packaging.

share. Here again, efforts have been made to adopt a marketing approach by increasing advertising budgets, yet decreasing margins are making such efforts almost impossible.

The need for structural change is recognised; however, with cut-throat competition, low productivity relative to the multinationals and low margins, there is little or no room for manoeuvre. As is the case with many Portuguese firms, the managers eye the future with apprehension, a sentiment most probably arising from a lack of knowledge and experience in the ways of modern competition, as opposed to an unwillingness to learn.

Young managers, sensing the need for change and for an injection of new blood, would like to take more drastic steps in the hope of being able to confront the new competitive situation rapidly being created by Europe's unification. However, as managers begin to grapple with the complexity of the developing environment, the proposals for change have come faster than their implementation.

The future of companies such as AL, regardless of where they may be, perhaps lies in the solution seen in the case of CMB Packaging (see Chapter 2) or FAI SpA (see Chapter 3): small and medium-sized companies joining larger multinationals to take advantage of such areas as research and development and project finance, all while maintaining the firm's original identity, be it internal or external.

The European Community is going to great lengths to control competition[3] and simultaneously promote small business through investment in specific projects as well as executive training programmes. However, a large amount of these funds, if not the majority, are being misused. Short-term greed is undermining the future prospects of industry throughout Europe and eating into taxpayers' salaries; but, so far, little has been done to control this effectively.

---

3. Articles 85 and 86 of the European Community statute forbid any actions which could in any way inhibit the competitive process across borders. Specifically, Article 85 aims to control agreements 'harmful' monopolies. The real power of the Community versus member states still remains ambiguous, as witnessed in the case of Tetra-Pak, the Swiss-based company, wishing to acquire a Swedish company.

It is an arguable point to say that 1992 is causing the restructuring and rationalisation of European industry. However, much as the Gulf War was an excuse for many companies to implement long-overdue rationalisation processes of their respective industries, '1992' can also be seen as merely a scapegoat for managers who are unwilling to recognise that large salaries and executive cars in exchange for inefficient management, poor business practices and cultural myopia are no longer the order of the day.

12 Concluding Remarks

European Corporate Strategy: Heading for 2000 can by no means pretend to be an exhaustive evaluation of the state of Europe's companies, large and small. However, the glimpse given does allow some insight into the challenges and opportunities being faced across the European continent, be it in Scandinavia, The Netherlands or Portugal, among the most important of which are:

- the elimination of the traditional competitive advantages, such as protected access to technology and markets;
- an ever more sophisticated and international consumer; and
- European deregulation.

This said, is a sample of nine companies and one industry overview really large enough to draw general conclusions regarding the readiness of Europe's managers to face the future? In and of itself, most would justifiably say 'no'. However, I believe that certain conclusions *can* be drawn, based on the fact that the research carried out involved countless interviews throughout Europe with individuals in political and academic as well as business sectors. The extent of these interviews, added to work experience, has provided me with a more global view of the overall situation and it is precisely such a view that I believe to be essential in preparing for the years ahead and the new century which lies beyond.

Such a global vision is distinctly lacking among politicians and governments; however, I believe that managers are becoming more aware of it. For the time being, Europe's governments are still entangled in endless EC debates over how to proceed towards a unified market and whether or not to proceed at all towards the creation of a 'United States of Europe'. While debating such issues, they continue to meddle in their internal economies, hoping that the powers-that-be will not notice – thus far, a highly valid assumption when speaking of the EC bureaucracy. Widespread industry subsidies as seen in the airline industry; technological barriers such as occur in information technology and other 'sensitive' areas; and import and export quotas as witnessed in textiles, and so on, all contribute to the maintenance of uncompetitive companies and industries. Such policies, while gaining votes in the short run, ultimately do harm to all concerned as they fail to attack seriously the root of the problem: the restructuring of a macroeconomy that is becoming increasingly global and orientated towards services rather than industry and that is generally acknowledged to be heading into areas previously uncharted. Such a challenge requires:

1. The qualified and in-depth training of individuals whose characteristics will be, among others, flexibility and polyvalence – training that should begin in the school and not as an afterthought in the factory.
2. The promotion of private-sector incentives that will allow managers to 'feel' their way in the years to come without having to worry excessively about legislation created in a world which is daily diminishing. Managers are increasingly aware that the competitive advantages of the future are not those that have been in operation in the post-Second World War era and they are also aware that most companies will need help to survive and to redefine the rules. However, as long as governments, both national and supranational, continue to apply double standards when judging competition,[1] favouring short-term as opposed to long-term solutions, then the managers' already difficult task will become almost impossible.

However, despite the often unhelpful government interference, Europe's managers *are* increasingly aware that their future success will rely on partnerships, and joint research and development projects; a willingness to adapt to new situations and to meet client needs; a willingness to make long-term investments in their staff; and on cultural flexibility. In all of these, I believe it can be

---

1. Numerous examples have been given throughout the book, most notably in the transport industry, though one can identify similar situations in textiles, agriculture, the steel industry and car manufacturing.

said that great strides are being made: the number of cross-cultural mergers and acquisitions have increased and continue to do so; more companies are investing in continuing professional education; increasing numbers of smaller companies are seeking partnerships, be they informal or well defined; and more and more senior managers are realising that a global view of competition and of the market, from both an industry and a geographical point of view, is essential to understand, evaluate and meet the demands of changing consumer tastes.

The one area where European managers are still weak, however, and this despite an increase in international activity, is in cultural flexibility. Europe is still too permeated by historical and cultural myopia that can have only a negative effect on relations, be they personal or professional. While there is talk of a united Europe, the number of independence movements is increasing (Catalunya, Basque country, Bolzano, Belgian Flanders, and, outside the EC, Slovenia, Croatia, to name only a few) and with it a renewed hostility towards ethnic groups. British companies still believe that, when working with a company from 'the Continent', they are actually doing that company a favour, the Dutch would rather not work with the Belgians or the Germans, the French would rather not work with anyone at all, and so on. While these generalisations may not apply as much to the multinationals and the larger companies, they do definitely apply to the smaller enterprises, the precise units that can make the most of cross-border activity and co-operation.

The companies selected for this book serve as an indication of what can be done, what has been done and what still needs to be accomplished in the decade that precedes the dawning of the new millenium.

Further Reading

Aaker, D.A., *Strategic Marketing Management* (New York: John Wiley and Sons, 1988).

Burgaud, D. and P. Mourier, *Euromarketing* (Paris: Les Editions d'Organisation, 1989).

Cecchini, P., *1992 – The European Challenge* (London: Wildwood House, 1989).

Cravers, D.W., *Strategic Management* (Boston, Mass.: Irwin Publishers, 1987)

Crespy, Guy, *Stratégies et Compétitivité dans l'Industrie Mondiale* (Paris: Economica, 1988).

Drew, John, *Europe 1992 – Developing an Active Company Approach to the European Market* (London: Whurr Publications, 1988).

Dudley, James, *1992 – Strategies for the Single Market* (London: Kogan Page, 1989).

Featherstone, K., *The Successful Manager's Guide to 1992* (London: Fontana, 1990).

Joffre, P. and G. Koenig, *L'Euro-entreprise* (Paris: Economica, 1989).

Silva, M. and B. Sjogren, *Europe 1992 and the New World* Power (London: Fontana, 1990)

Taylor, C., *1992 – Facts and Challenges* (London: Industrial Society, 1989).

Veljanowski, C., *Whose Europe?* (London: Institute of Economic Affairs, 1989).

Business Guide to the EC Initiatives (Brussels: American Chamber of Commerce, 1990).

Europe in Numbers (Brussels: EC Documentation, 1990).

Panorama of EC Industry (Brussels: EC Industrial Economic Services, 1990).

Index